AF243797

The Last General

THE LAST GENERAL

BEN B. WALTON

WRITER'S PROOF

Published by Writer's Proof,
an imprint of Miglior Press

Athens, Georgia

www.migliorpress.com

ISBN 978-0-9822726-3-3

Printed in the United States of America

To my wife,
Judy,
and granddaughter,
Savannah

Accept the things to which fate binds you, and love the people to whom fate brings you together, but do so with all your heart.

—Marcus Aurelius

It is more important how a man meets his fate than what it is.

—Wilhelm von Humboldt

CONTENTS

PREFACE

For a five-year period from 1998–2002, I worked for an organization headquartered in Atlanta, Georgia, that provides training services to companies located throughout the state. My home, however, was then and is now in Montgomery, Alabama, a distance of 180 miles to the southwest. Since this was too far for a daily work commute, I rented an apartment in Atlanta and would drive there from Montgomery on Monday mornings, spend the week working, and return home to Montgomery on Friday evenings.

Interstate 85 connects Atlanta and Montgomery, and at the mid-point, the Chattahoochee river divides the two states. Traveling south on I-85, just before crossing the bridge and entering Alabama, there is a final exit going to West Point, Georgia. For years, each week as I traveled home, I would see this exit and look down the road that ran west for half a mile, then curved out of site. I wondered about the town of West Point. How big was it? What did it look like? How did it get its name? Why would people want to live there? I often thought of stopping to visit, but it was always late in the day—plus I was tired and still had ninety miles more to travel to reach home—so I never stopped to visit the community. One day, however, all that would change.

In 2003, I retired from my job in Atlanta and could now spend all my time in Montgomery. However, my retirement was short-lived. In 2004, Hyundai decided to build a plant in Montgomery. Not long after, I was offered a job managing the Hyundai training center, and I accepted.

Eighteen months later, KIA, a division of Hyundai, decided to build an automobile plant in Georgia. I was asked to serve as a training consultant. I agreed and once again would be working in Georgia. The plant site was in West Point. Now I would get to visit the town and get the answers to all the questions that had been on my mind for so many years.

Over the next two years, I was able to visit the community frequently, and the more I learned of the town's rich history, the more I wanted to know. I learned there had been a Confederate fort, Fort Tyler, located at the edge of town, and one of the last major battles of the Civil War was fought there on Easter Sunday, April 16, 1865, and Fort Tyler was the last Confederate fort captured by the Union Army. I also learned that the fort was commanded by Brigadier General Robert Charles Tyler, a bold and courageous soldier with a life full of interesting experiences. What I learned about General Tyler's life became the basis for this book, a work of creative nonfiction.

Ben Walton

CHAPTER ONE

4:15 a.m., January 14, 1859, Rivas, Nicaragua. Lieutenant Robert Tyler peered into the darkness, trying unsuccessfully to see how many soldiers he had remaining and evaluate their fighting condition. He had entered the battle two days ago with 327 fighters, a combination of American mercenaries and Nicaraguan militia. From the beginning, they had been at a great disadvantage, outnumbered four to one by a far superior force of trained professional Costa Rican soldiers. Tyler's men had made up for their lack of experience with courage and daring as the fighting raged almost continuously, with little time for rest, food, or water. The intense fighting and relentless heat beating down on them from the scorching sun had taken a heavy toll on his force. His men had gradually been forced backwards on the battlefield and were now taking cover in what was little more than a slight depression along the edge of a trail.

Gradually, streaks of orange and yellow began to appear in the eastern sky, indicating the long, hot night was finally coming to an end. A soft grey dawn silently rolled across the fields, and now the lieutenant could see the men in the ravine with him. He counted forty-seven soldiers still alive—fourteen were Americans, including himself, and thirty-three Nicaraguans—but most important, with the light, Lieutenant Tyler could now also see the terrible condition of his men. They had fought valiantly against great odds, and now they were exhausted. Many had abandoned their weapons and were staring at the ground with glazed, red-rimmed eyes. Even the lookouts had left their positions and joined the group of exhausted soldiers. The lieutenant knew then that the fighting was over; it would be futile for him to attempt to rouse the men to repel another charge by the enemy. Suddenly, as if on cue, 100 Costa Rican soldiers appeared at the top of the ravine, their weapons pointing down at the men.

A Costa Rican officer walked slowly to the front of the captives and said in Spanish, *"Usted ahora es mi cautivos."* (You are now my captives.) *"Todos ustedes deben tener es sus pies."* (All of you must get on your feet.)

The men in the ditch slowly rose to their feet and formed a ragged line.

"Que vas a hacer con nostros?" (What will you do with us?) asked one of the Nicaraguan soldiers.

"Usted va a tener in la ciudad." (You are going to be taken into town.) *"Y manana que se ejector."* (And tomorrow you will all be executed.) *"Y nos asequraremos,"* (And we will make sure), he added with a smile, *"los americanos seran los primeros a ser fusilado"* (the Americans will be shot first.)

The prisoners were marched to the small town of Rivas, trailing a cloud of dust as they made their way down the dirt road. A few of the townspeople stopped and silently stared as the captives walked by. They approached a row of small, rundown wooden shacks, and several of the men were put in each of them. Because he was an officer, the lieutenant was put in one of the shacks by himself. He looked around and saw there was only a table, a chair, and a wooden cot. With only one small window, the room was already hot. Tyler walked to the cot, lay down on the hard wooden slats, and stared at the ceiling. He drifted off to sleep, occasionally slapping at a mosquito when it lit on his face. After a few hours, he was awakened when an old woman brought in a bucket of warm water and a ladle and offered him a drink. She left the room and returned with a bowl of beans and rice and a hunk of hard bread. He grabbed the bread and sopped it into the mixture and began to eat. The lieutenant had eaten little in two days, and he felt better after his nap and the food and water. He sat on the edge of the bunk and wiped the sweat from his forehead as he tried to think of a way out of his situation, wondering if this was to be his last day alive.

Rivas is a small fishing village in the southwest corner of Nicaragua. Located 100 miles south of Managua, the capital, and just a few miles north of the Costa Rican border, the town is bordered on the west by the Pacific Ocean and on the east by Lago de Nicaragua, (Lake Nicaragua), the tenth largest freshwater lake in the world. Rivas is situated on a narrow finger of land separating the two great bodies of water. The town was settled centuries ago by local Indian tribes. For hundreds of years, the Indians had existed quietly there, living on the abundant fish from the lake and the Pacific and some ranching and agriculture. They raised a few head of cattle and planted crops of plantains, sugar cane, rice, and grenadine. In the evenings, the Indians would look out over the quiet lake and pray to Maderas, a dormant volcano located on the island of Ometrepe, that jutted out of the middle of the lake. The volcano looked down on the village and was thought to bring an abundance of good fortune. The little village had existed for centuries with scant attention or interest. Recently, however, all that had changed.

Now, the villagers had a new and lucrative source of income. Their good fortune came from transportation, in the form of carrying travelers and their accompanying baggage between Lake Nicaragua and the Pacific Ocean. What had brought this new interest to Rivas was the discovery of gold in California. The resulting gold rush had people traveling by every means available. The slowest and most perilous way of travel was overland. The only other means was by ship, a long and arduous 1,500 mile journey down the east coast of South America, around Cape Horn and then on up to the California coast. "Rounding the Horn" was a treacherous journey around the southernmost point of South America. Cape Horn was known as one of the most hazardous ship routes in the world. Sailors referred to the area as the "sailor's graveyard" or "cape of treacherous storms." There was always a significant risk of being driven into rocks from the fierce winds, and large waves and icebergs were an additional hazard. With the discovery of the "Nicaraguan Canal," travelers could board a steamship on the East Coast and travel to Greytown, Nicaragua, via the Caribbean Sea. There they could change to a smaller, flat-bottom, shallow-draft steamboat, and travel the 300 miles up the San Juan River that separated Nicaragua and Costa Rica, cross Lake Nicaragua, and offload at Rivas. Local Nicaraguans would then transport the travelers and their baggage the twelve miles overland, where they would board waiting large steamboats and continue on to San Francisco. The discovery of this new route shortened the trip by over 7,500 miles.

The hours wore on as Lieutenant Tyler sat on the wooden bunk and pondered his fate. The sun, now directly overhead, baked the little town and its inhabitants. Time moved slowly in the little room, with the only noise the buzz of flies, as they flew in and out of the small window.

Suddenly, in mid-afternoon, his guard brushed back the dirty blanket that served as the door to the shack. He waved to the lieutenant and growled, "*Ven conmigo.*" (Come with me.)

Taken completely by surprise, the lieutenant grabbed his hat, stood up, and followed the guard out the door. Once outside, he breathed deeply and noticed it was cooler, even under the mid-day sun. He prayed they had not decided to move his execution to today, as he was guided down the dirt street by his guard, passing several more shacks. They arrived at a two-story, clay-brick structure that appeared to serve as the town's official government building, stepped inside and moved down a long, dark hallway. The guard pointed to one of the doorways and motioned for him to enter. As he opened the door and walked into the room, it took a few seconds for his eyes to adjust to the dim light of one small lamp. He saw a table and two chairs and a man sitting at the table, staring at him. Tyler noticed the man was slight in build and had a pale complexion. He definitely was not from this area of the country and had not previously experienced a rough life.

The man stood and introduced himself: "Hello, my name is Albert Jennings Fountain. Please take a seat."

Tyler pulled the chair out and sat down, as he continued to stare at Fountain, wondering what this was all about.

"I'm a reporter for the *Sacramento Union*," said Fountain. "Your captors have given me permission to interview you before your execution. If you cooperate and talk to me, I can only promise you I will take your story back to the United States and share it with the American people."

"I suppose I have nothing to lose," said Tyler. "Just what do you want to know?"

Fountain withdrew a tablet and pen from a pouch and laid them on the table. "Well, let's start with where you are from, where you were born, and where you grew up."

Tyler leaned back in his chair and began to talk. "I was born in a little town just east of Memphis, Tennessee, in 1833. My mother died when I was just a baby. My father moved the family to Baltimore while I was still very young, and we lived there for several years. My father remarried and moved the family to Alabama, but I was left in Baltimore to live with my uncle. After I had grown up, my uncle died, and I decided to travel west to see California and seek my fortune."

"What brought you down here to Nicaragua to fight in a war so far from home?" asked Fountain.

"One day, I read an article in the newspaper about a General William Walker and his plans to conduct a filibustering expedition down in Mexico and forcibly take over an area and declare it as United States territory, and he was recruiting mercenaries for his venture. Pay was to be a portion of the captured land. Walker was from near my hometown in Tennessee, and since I had no family or other ties to keep me in America, I sought him out and signed on."

"How did the venture go in Mexico?" asked Fountain.

"It went well at first. We traveled down to Baja California and captured La Paz, the capital of that area. Walker renamed it the Republic of Sonora, and declared himself president," said Tyler.

"Then what happened?"

"Well, our problems started after a few months. We began to run out of supplies and couldn't get them replaced. We were only a few hundred strong, and, eventually, the Mexican Army overwhelmed us. We had to retreat back to California."

"What did you do after that?" asked Fountain, continuing to take notes.

"General Walker was not going to be deterred. He knew that there was an ongoing civil war down here in Nicaragua, so he made contact with the Nicaraguan Democratic Party and got permission to bring down a group of mercenaries (disguised as colonists) to overtake the country. Then he promoted himself Governor of Nicaragua."

"Why were you in a battle with the Army of Costa Rica?" asked Fountain.

"As you know, Costa Rica borders Nicaragua just a few miles to the south of here. Costa Rica has been a long-time enemy of Nicaragua and believes it has the rights to this area of the country. They believe Nicaragua is in a weakened state and see now as the time to take control of land that is rightly theirs."

Fountain put down his pen and stared at Tyler for a moment. "And now you will die," he said softly. "How do you want the American people to remember you?"

Tyler thought for a minute, trying to understand the

enormity of the question he was just asked. "I suppose I want people to know that I was brave and loyal to the men fighting with me, and that I died having no regrets for my actions," he said.

Fountain stood and offered his hand to Tyler. As they shook hands, he looked Tyler in the eye and said, "I promise I will do my best to get your story to the American people. May God be with you."

Tyler nodded, but had nothing more to say. He turned and walked out the door.

William Walker, a very intelligent, controversial, and complex individual, was born in Nashville, Tennessee, in 1824, and graduated, at age fourteen, *summa cum laude* from the University of Nashville. He then traveled throughout Europe for two years, studying medicine at the universities of Edinburgh, Heidelberg, Gottingen, and Paris. At nineteen, he received a medical degree from the University of Pennsylvania and practiced medicine briefly in Philadelphia before moving to New Orleans to study law. He practiced law for a short time before becoming part owner and editor of the newspaper the *New Orleans Crescent*. In 1848, Walker moved to San Francisco, California, where he worked as a journalist and fought three duels and was wounded in two of them.

Around this time, he developed the plan of privately conquering vast regions of Central America in order to create states ruled by white English people. Such campaigns were then known as "filibustering." (The Spanish word "filibuster" means pirate or buccaneer. In the mid-nineteenth century it was used to describe the actions of adventurers who tried to take control of various Caribbean, Mexican, and Central American territories by force.) The American public enjoyed reading about the thrilling adventures of filibusters. Notwithstanding the fact they were in violation of the Neutrality Act of 1794, which made it illegal to wage war against another country at peace with the United States, at the time there were many Americans that supported "Manifest Destiny," a belief that the United States was destined, even divinely ordained, to extend its territories across the American continent.

Walker's first venture was in Baja California in 1853, where he led a group of mercenaries, men recruited mainly from Kentucky and Tennessee. He took the fighters to La Paz, the Republic of lower California, and installed himself as president. The Mexican government quickly forced Walker and his men to retreat back to California, where he was put on trial for conducting an illegal war that violated American neutrality laws. In an era of the Manifest Destiny doctrine, his filibustering project had been popular in the southern and western United States. It took the jury only eight minutes to acquit him.

The failure in Mexico did not deter Walker. His next expedition took him to Central America, where he had learned there was a civil war raging in the republic of Nicaragua. Walker contracted with the Nicaraguan president to bring several hundred mercenaries to serve the Democratic Republic. On September 4, 1855, Walker's forces defeated the Nicaraguan National Army, conquered the capital of Granada, and took control of the country. As commander of the army, Walker set himself up as president of Nicaragua.

Walker's downfall and ultimate demise was due in large part to making an enemy of Cornelius Vanderbilt, an extremely wealthy American. Vanderbilt had made his vast fortune in railroads and shipping, and when the California gold rush began in 1849, he switched from regional steamboat lines to ocean-going steamships. It was "Commodore" Vanderbilt who discovered the Nicaraguan Canal. Also, he founded the Accessory Transit Company and negotiated transit rights with Nicaragua to provide steamboat transportation across Nicaragua using Lake Nicaragua and the San Juan River. When Walker took over the country, Vanderbilt's enemies convinced Walker to revoke his rights and confiscate his steamboats and equipment. Vanderbilt retaliated by negotiating with Costa Rica and other Central American countries to declare war on Walker. William Walker was defeated by the four other Central American nations and eventually executed by a firing squad on the order of local Honduran authorities.

CHAPTER TWO

With the arrival of evening, it began to cool slightly in the shack. The guard had brought a small candle to light the room, and the old woman brought some hard bread and a dish of rice covered with fried fish. Lieutenant Tyler dipped the bread in the bowl and ate as he pondered his fate. His chance of escape was almost zero with the guard sitting just outside the entrance facing the door. The guard would notice any movement to the opening. The only other opening was a window, but it was so small that he could not get his body through. Tyler smiled grimly, thinking that this was a terrible way to spend his last night alive. He lay on the cot and tried to think of some way out of his predicament.

The evening wore on, until suddenly, the guard appeared at the entrance and motioned for Tyler to follow him. What now, he thought, as they retraced their steps from the afternoon and again entered the two-story building. They proceeded to the same little room that he had been in before, and he entered, adjusting his eyes to the dim light. Albert Fountain sat at the table, in the same place as he had been earlier in the afternoon. This time he looked different. Before, he had seemed calm and quiet. But now his face was flushed, and he was clearly agitated and nervous. He motioned for Tyler to sit down and immediately began to speak.

"There have been some changes since we talked this afternoon," Albert said.

"What is it?" asked Tyler.

"General Walker has placed a bounty on my head; he is offering a reward for my death."

Tyler was surprised. "And why would he do that?"

"Apparently, he is upset by a recent article I wrote."

"What was in the article?" asked Tyler.

"I declared that the general had plans to institute slavery in Nicaragua and the other Central American countries he planned to conquer."

"Is that true?"

"Yes, he has stated that is his intention."

"I am sorry for your circumstances, but what has it to do with me?"

"I have an offer for you—one that will help us both, if you are interested."

"And what is your offer?"

"I have a plan that will free you from your capture and help you escape."

"I'm very interested. Tell me more."

"I have brought clothes for disguises for both of us. All we have to do is make it safely through the village and to a boat that will take us to San Carlos."

"And why would you help me escape?"

"As you can see, I am small and frail. In case we are challenged, I need your protection."

"Are you forgetting there are guards outside waiting for me?"

"No, they are gone. Stick your head out the door, and you will see they are not there."

Tyler did so and noted there were no guards in sight. "How did you do this?" he asked.

"Cordova," said Albert. "I bought them off. These people are very poor, and money always works."

"I have also procured passage on a boat that leaves very soon. We need to be on our way, or we will not reach it in time."

"Your plan may not work, but it's much better than sitting in a room, waiting to be shot. You can count me in," said Tyler.

Fountain pulled some clothing from a bag. "Here is some women's clothing. Put it on."

Tyler took the clothes and said, "I am sure that you will be able to pass as a female in the darkness, but what about me? I'm six feet tall and have a mustache."

"I thought of that," said Fountain. "Here is a kerchief. If anyone approaches, turn your head and put the kerchief to your mouth to cover your mustache. We must hurry; the boat will not wait for us."

They both donned dresses, put bonnets on their heads, and slipped out the door.

Fortunately, there was no moon that night and little movement in the town as Tyler and Fountain moved cautiously down the dirt trails and pathways connecting the buildings in the village. When they saw someone approaching, they moved into the nearby trees and bushes and were not observed. They made it to the edge of the lake and were met by a skiff and two men that were to take them across the lake to the village of San Carlos, where a steamboat was waiting to transport them down the San Juan River. The two escapees were met with smiles as they proceeded to get in the boat in their dresses and bonnets.

They quickly discarded their costumes as the boat quietly moved out into the lake. The small steamboat moved quickly on the lake and created only small ripples as they hurried along. In less than four hours, the lights of a village came into view and seemed to become larger as they approached the pier. Tyler and Fountain scanned the area for anyone that might present a danger, but all appeared quiet and peaceful. The boat pulled up to the dock, and one of the men grabbed a rope and tied it to a post. The two passengers quickly jumped onto the dock and moved to the shore. They could see a steamboat with a lighted kerosene lamp on its bow at a nearby pier, so they went over to see if it was their transportation down the river. It was.

CHAPTER THREE

With the two men safely aboard, the small steamboat moved away from the San Carlos pier at dawn and began its journey down the San Juan River. Its destination was Greytown, 300 miles downriver on the Carribean sea. There were only a few passengers on board, since the majority of traffic was in the other direction, the way to California and its gold. Fountain and Tyler sat on the deck and watched the shoreline as the boat slowly moved down the river. In order to navigate the numerous bends, the shallow areas, and occasional rapids, the small steamboats could only make about three miles an hour.

The San Juan River is a timeless passageway through dense tropical rain forest from Central America's grandest lake to the Caribbean Sea. The men gazed at the banks of the river and marveled at all the animal life they saw. There were crocodiles sunning themselves on the flats, large turtles slowly moving to and from the water, giant anteaters, an occasional jaguar, and, high overhead, spider monkeys swinging from tree to tree as they followed the boat southward. Tropical birds of all colors flew in the quiet air above them, as butterflies flitted around the colorful bushes and flowers. Mark Twain once traveled on the river and described it in his notebook as "an earthly paradise," one of the most enjoyable and rewarding rain-forest experiences available anywhere. Among all the colorful sights, it was easy to forget that the water divided two countries that had fought for many years over ownership and rights to travel on the river. Many bloody battles had been fought between Nicaragua and Costa Rica over who would have the final say for control of the waters.

At various points along the San Juan, it becomes shallow, and at other times there are rapids. Therefore, only smaller shallow-draft boats can safely navigate around the obstacles. The river was first discovered by pirates that roamed the Caribbean, and they used it for hiding and for trading goods with the locals. During the period that Spain controlled Central America, the Spanish built a series of twelve forts along the banks of the river, and they used these forts to fight invading pirates, buccaneers, and filibusters. During the early nineteenth century, they also used the forts during the hostile years between Spain and England.

As the boat slowly made its way toward Greytown, the two men laid on the deck and discussed their plans for the future. Fountain had decided to go out West, perhaps New Mexico, to start a new career. Tyler, on the other hand, had decided to go back to Tennessee, where he was born. He knew that talk of a war between the states was increasing, and if it happened, he would join the army and defend the South. When the boat finally reached its destination, they wished each other the best of fortune and parted ways.

Albert Fountain was born Albert Jennings on Staten Island, New York, on October 23, 1838. His parents were Solomon Jennings, a sea captain, and Catherine de la Fontaine. While Albert was still young, his father disappeared after his ship went down in rough seas. As a young man, Albert changed his last name in honor of his mother, and from that point on he was known as Albert Jennings Fountain. Fountain claimed to be a graduate of Columbia College, but there are no records of his attendance. As a young man, he traveled the world and then settled in Sacramento, California. There, he prospected for gold and hauled supplies to mining camps. He took a job as a reporter for the *Sacramento Union* and traveled to Nicaragua to report on the filibuster of General William Walker. In Nicaragua, he narrowly escaped execution by Walkers' fighters when he reported that Walker planned to introduce slavery to the middle-America region.

Fountain returned to California and began studying law. He was only days away from being admitted to the California Bar when Union recruiters came to Sacramento, and he immediately enlisted in the Union army and was commissioned as an officer in the California Column. He fought in the Rio Grande Valley territory to gain control from the Confederates. Later, he was assigned to Fort Bliss, Texas, to fight both Confederates and Indians. By early 1866, Fountain's military service ended, and he was discharged as a captain. By then he was married, and he moved his wife and two children to El Paso and began his law career.

In 1869, Fountain won a seat in the Texas senate. He worked in the senate to benefit west Texas, serving on the Indian affairs, frontier protection, and public lands committees. He also served as majority leader of the senate. For a period, he also served as lieutenant governor, since that office was vacant during his second session in the legislature. Fountain had radical Republican views that angered Texas Democrats, and he was challenged to several duels, killing at least one man.

His radical views may have also lead to his disappearance

and presumed murder. In 1873, Fountain decided to move his family to Mesilla, New Mexico. He became a lawyer in Mesilla, where he defended such historical figures as Billy the Kid and Bronco Sue Dodson. He was then appointed assistant district attorney and became known for his impressive prosecutions. He was also a militia officer in the wars with the Apaches, reached the rank of colonel, and would be known as Colonel Fountain for the remainder of his life. On February 1, 1896, Fountain and his eight-year-old son, Henry, disappeared near White Sands as they were on their way back to Mesilla from Las Cruces, New Mexico.

Fountain was returning from prosecuting two cattle rustlers. The two men had been defended by Albert B. Fall. Fall later became a senator and befriended Governor William H. Harrison of Ohio, who later became president of the United States. Harrison appointed Fall as secretary of the interior, and Fall became involved in the notorious Teapot Dome scandal. Fall and several others schemed to steal and sell the oil reserves from Teapot Dome, Wyoming. Fall was later prosecuted and was the first presidential cabinet member to serve jail time. Many people believe he was behind the murder and disappearance of Fountain and his son, but no solid proof was ever found against him. Their bodies were never found.

CHAPTER FOUR

Two Confederate soldiers sat at a small table in the middle of a dirt street in Nashville, Tennessee. In front of them was a long, single-formation line of young men and boys. One of the soldiers was a sergeant, and he talked to each person as the other soldier, a corporal, made notes on a tablet. After a discussion lasting a few minutes, the person being interviewed moved off to the side of the street and waited with the others that had been interviewed. The line moved slowly, and the sun got hotter as it rose overhead. Occasionally, the sergeant would take off his hat, wipe his forehead with his sleeve, spit tobacco juice in the street, and then place his hat back on his head. Robert Tyler stood in the line, waiting patiently, as he slowly moved forward. Eventually, he was standing in front of the table, facing the two soldiers.

"Your name?" asked the sergeant.

"Robert Charles Tyler," he replied, and the corporal dutifully wrote his name on the tablet.

"Where and when born?"

"Near Memphis, Tennessee, on July 17, 1833."

"Let's see now, that makes you how old?" drawled the sergeant.

"Twenty-seven years and ten months," said Tyler.

The sergeant squinted at him for a few seconds and then said, "You're a little old to be volunteering as a recruit. You see those other fellows over there? They're all about sixteen to nineteen years old."

"That's all right. I still want to join up," said Tyler.

The sergeant spit another gob on the street, and then asked, "Are you of your own free will volunteering to fight for the Confederacy?"

"I am," said Tyler.

"And do you pledge to fight and give your life, if need be, in support of the Confederate Army of Tennessee?"

"I will do so," said Tyler.

And, finally, do you agree to abide by the orders and dictates of Jefferson Davis, President of the Confederate States of America?"

"I do," said Tyler.

"Well then, I want to welcome you as a private in the Confederate Army of Tennessee."

"Thank you," said Tyler, smiling.

"Now go on over there to the side of the street and wait with the other privates," said the sergeant. "As soon as we finish up here, we will take you all out to camp on the outskirts of town. And we'll get you fitted up right with a uniform and weapon."

Tyler gave the surprised sergeant a proper salute, turned on his heel, and walked over to the side of the street where the other new recruits were waiting.

Private Tyler's previous fighting experience and leadership abilities quickly became evident to the officers of the Army of Tennessee, and he was given an officer commission and promoted to the rank of major. His first combat action was at Shiloh, Tennessee, in one of the deadliest battles of the war. The battle of Shiloh, the first major battle of the war, occurred on April 6–7, 1862. Shiloh was one of the most critical battles in American history. Many of the most famous figures of the Civil War—including Grant, Sherman, Johnston, Beauregard, Buell, and Bragg, Commander of the Army of Tennessee—fought there.

On April 6, in the first light of dawn, Confederates overran one Union division, and there was savage fighting around Shiloh Church. Casualties around this killing ground were immense. Shiloh's first day of slaughter included the death of General Johnston, considered one of the Confederate army's finest leaders.

That evening, Tyler and the chaplain walked among the troops as they were eating their evening meal and preparing for the night. Tyler noticed many of the soldiers had graphite and paper, and they were writing notes and attaching them to their clothing. Tyler turned to the chaplain and asked, "What are the notes for?"

"Sometimes they will give me the notes to mail home for them, but often they just pin them on their clothing, for tomorrow they know they will die, and these notes contain their last words to loved ones," he replied. The chaplain looked at Tyler and asked, "Do you want to pen a note to your loved ones?"

"Chaplain, I have no family or loved ones to send a message to, so I have no note to prepare." Tyler then turned and walked away.

The next day, April 7, General Grant renewed the fighting with an aggressive counterattack. Taken by surprise, General Beauregard rallied 30,000 of the Confederates and mounted a fierce defense, inflicting heavy casualties on the Federals. Grant, however, had more strength in numbers and, in the end, prevailed. The Confederates retreated and withdrew from the area during the night. A total of 23,746 men were killed or wounded at Shiloh. The magnitude of this loss brought a shocking realization to both sides: this war would not end quickly.

Tyler's next major action was on September 18–20, 1863, at Chickamauga, Tennessee. This battle was one in a series known as the Chattanooga Campaign. The Confederate forces held Chattanooga, Tennessee, a city vitally important because it served as a Confederate rail center, and it also guarded the path to Atlanta and the deep South.

General Grant ordered General Rosecrans to seize Chattanooga, which was under the guard of General Bragg and the Army of Tennessee. On September 18, General Bragg marched north and contacted the Union forces. Bragg's goal was to take the crossings over Chickamauga creek. Tyler commanded a regiment at Chickamauga. At the end of the first day's action, he walked among his troops, providing words of praise and encouragement for what he knew would be fierce action the next day. At dusk, as Tyler looked out over the fields, a bugler began to sound "Taps." The slow, melancholy notes always had a sad, but settling, effect on him, and he softly repeated the lyrics to the music as it was played:

Day is done,
Gone the sun,
From the lakes,
From the hills,
From the sky,
All is well,
Safely rest,
God is near.
Thanks and praise,
For our days,
'Neath the sun,
'Neath the stars,
'Neath the sky,
As we go,
This we know,
God is near.

The next day, September 19, General Bragg's men pounded, but did not break through, the Union line. Bragg continued his assault, eventually driving one third of the Union army from the field. Tyler fought valiantly at Chickamauga, even single-handedly dragging a Yankee cannon back to the Confederate lines. There were 35,000 killed or wounded during the fighting. For his heroic deeds, Tyler was given a battlefield promotion to colonel.

The battle of Missionary Ridge, another battle that was part of the Chattanooga Campaign, was fought on November 25, 1863. It followed the Union victory the day before at the battle of Lookout Mountain, located ten miles south of Chattanooga. The fighting began that morning as General

Sherman attempted to capture the northern end of Missionary Ridge, but his force was stopped by fierce resistance from the Confederates. Colonel Tyler commanded a brigade during the fighting at Missionary Ridge. During the day, General Grant continued to reinforce his troops that were attacking the Confederate defenses, and they began to gain ground. In the afternoon, the Union soldiers reached the crest of the ridge, and it was at this time that Colonel Tyler was severely wounded. With a final assault, the Union forces reached the summit. General Bragg's forces withdrew south toward Dalton, Georgia. The Union had successfully driven off Braggs's entire army. The defeat at Missionary Ridge and loss of Chattanooga were a severe blow to the Confederate cause. A vital line of communications was also lost, and now Sherman could move to split the Confederacy further with his Atlanta campaign and march to the sea.

CHAPTER FIVE

Two corpsmen brought Colonel Tyler into the surgical tent on a stretcher. He was obviously in severe pain from his leg wound and almost unconscious from loss of blood. Someone had thought to apply a tourniquet to his leg above the wound, but blood still seeped down his leg. The surgical tent was loud and chaotic due to the large number of wounded; they were being cared for by male nurses and doctors. Tables were located in the four corners of the tent, and surgeons and assistants were all busy operating on the soldiers. Due to the heat, most of the medical staff were stripped to the waist and splattered with blood. A cart had been backed up to the rear of the tent and mangled limbs were discarded on the cart as soon as they were surgically removed.

One of the surgeons motioned for the corpsmen to place Colonel Tyler on a table. The surgeon pulled off the colonel's left boot and, using a large pair of scissors, cut away the trousers and exposed the mangled flesh. He needed only a minute to examine the wound and determine what must be done. Colonel Tyler's left leg just below the knee was completely shattered. His lower leg and foot were hanging on by just a few shreds of skin.

The Surgeon knew immediately that the Colonel had been struck by a minnie ball that had hit the large leg bone and shattered it into a thousand pieces. There was no way his leg could be saved.

For nearly 200 years, soldiers had been issued a smooth-bore musket as their standard weapon. As the word implies, the smooth-bore musket did not have spiraling rifle grooves cut into the bore. A round lead ball rattled around as it was discharged out of the barrel, making it terribly inaccurate. Most of the muskets didn't even have aiming sights. Because of the muskets' inaccuracies, military strategy was to mass troops into lines and fire coordinated volleys, in hopes that some of the round lead bullets would strike a target.

All that changed in 1845, when a French army captain named Claude-Etienne Minie invented the Minie ball, or minnie ball. Captain Minie designed a hollow, soft-lead, cone-shaped bullet that could be forced into the barrel of a rifle that contained spiral rifling groves. The spinning bullet exiting the barrel of the rifle greatly increased the distance and accuracy of the weapon, and the bullet would cause major damage when it smashed into a body. The accuracy of the weapon was further increased by adding aiming sights. A weapon that fired a minnie ball was the common firearm used by both Union and Confederate soldiers. The deadly effectiveness of the rifled musket loaded with a minnie ball is largely the reason for the Civil War's enormous casualty rates: over 400,000 Union and Confederate soldiers were killed and an additional 500,000 wounded. The minnie ball caused over ninety percent of the casualties.

Again, after his examination of Colonel Tyler's shattered leg, the surgeon knew that it had to be amputated. He went to a nearby shelf and took down a quart jug of clear liquid and uncorked the top.

"Drink this," he said, as he handed the jug to the colonel.

Tyler raised his head and took a large drink. He immediately began choking and coughing.

"That's corn liquor!" he gasped, as he tried to get back his breath.

"Yes, it is," said the surgeon. "We don't have any thing to give you to act as anesthesia, so this is the only thing we have to use. I'm going to have to operate on your leg, so drink all you can."

As Colonel Tyler began to understand the enormity of what was about to take place, he took the jug and gulped down several large swigs of the liquor. He was already very weak from loss of blood, and he continued to drink the alcohol. After a few minutes, his head dropped back on the table as he lost consciousness.

The surgeon had received eighteen months of medical training and had performed hundreds of amputations since he had entered military service, so he knew exactly what he must do to save the colonel's life. He grabbed a large knife and saw, poured some of the alcohol over them, and commenced to operate. First, he cut the flesh away from the wound area, leaving as much skin attached as possible. The colonel moaned occasionally, but remained unconscious. Next, the surgeon used the saw to sever the two major leg bones. He threw the severed leg and foot into the back of a nearby cart, which held a stack of arms and legs. He went to a corner of the tent that had a hot stove holding several red hot pokers. He grabbed one and applied it to the flesh of the leg where he had just operated. The hot poker cauterized and sealed the wound. Colonel Tyler groaned every few minutes from the pain. The surgeon took the flaps of skin and pulled them over the stub of leg. Using a large needle and catgut thread, he sewed the flaps tightly together, then poured some of the liquor over the sewn area. He loosened the tourniquet and checked to see if there was any bleeding and was relieved to see it remained dry. He took cotton cloth and bandaged the entire area, using twine to hold the cloth tightly on the stub of leg. The entire operation had taken only twenty minutes, and he knew there were many more wounded waiting for him.

The surgeon motioned for two orderlies to bring a stretcher.

"The colonel is going to require care and attention while he recuperates; you need to get him to his loved ones right away," he said.

"Sir, I don't think Colonel Tyler has any kin," said one of the men.

The surgeon looked outside and saw two ambulance wagons loaded with wounded soldiers that had recently been treated.

"Where are they taking those soldiers?" he asked.

"They're going to go down to Georgia, to recuperate," the soldier said.

"Well, load the colonel on one of the wagons; they can take him, too," he ordered.

CHAPTER SIX

The sun had set and dusk was fast approaching as the two ambulance buckboards loaded with wounded soldiers moved slowly down the main street of West Point, Georgia. The drivers pulled the horses to a stop in front of some houses, and several women came out to help. With words of encouragement, a woman assisted each one of the wounded soldiers as he got off the wagon and then supported him in moving as he was guided into a home. Sarah Bradford stood at the edge of the road and watched the proceedings. Finally, there was only one remaining soldier lying in the wagon, and he appeared to be unconscious.

"What about him?" she asked the two soldiers.

"That's the colonel," said one of the men. "He's been mostly out the whole trip. He's lost a leg, bled a lot, probably going to die."

Sarah grimaced, but spoke firmly to the men. "No, he's not going to die. Please bring him into my house, take him upstairs, and put him in the bed in the room at the end of the hall."

The soldiers rolled the colonel onto a crude stretcher and carried him into the house. Once he was placed on the bed and the men had left, Sarah noticed the awful smell. She dabbed some perfume onto a kerchief and held it to her nose. She opened a window on each side of the room, allowing a slight breeze to enter. Then she lit a kerosene lamp and held it close to the soldier to check his condition. He was dirty, smelly, and breathing in shallow sighs. Next, she went downstairs to the kitchen and got a glass of sweet tea, several wash cloths, and a pan of water. She returned to the bedroom, dipped one washcloth into the glass of tea, and put it to his mouth. Not wanting to choke him, she only brushed the wet cloth over his lips. After doing that for a few minutes, she began the distasteful task of cleaning him. First, she removed his shirt, pants, and the one boot and sock. Keeping the kerchief close to her nose, she used scissors to cut off his undershirt and shorts. Starting at his hairline, she began to bathe him. As she washed his face, she had to acknowledge that he was a very handsome man. He had dark, bushy eyebrows, long eyelashes, a patrician nose, mustache, and firm chin.

She was suddenly very sad and scared. Her eyes began to water as she prayed, "God, please don't let this man die." Sarah continued to hold the kerchief to her nose with one hand as she washed the rest of his body with the other. When she was finished bathing him, she took his dirty clothes and the pan of dirty water downstairs. She replaced the water in the pan and retrieved another wash cloth, some gauze, bandages, and pins. She returned to the bedroom, faced the open window, and took a deep breath. Sarah wasn't sure she could complete the next task, but started in. She began to cut away the bandages on the stump of the leg. She carefully removed all the bloody mess and was relieved to see that although there had been some bleeding, there did not appear to be any infection. "Thank you, God," she muttered, as she gently wiped away the dried blood.

After the initial revulsion of looking at the wound, she could see that the surgeon had done a fair job in covering the opening and sewing the flaps of skin. Sarah wiped the entire area, using witch hazel as an antiseptic, and then covered the area, first with gauze and then with cloth bandages. She pulled the cloth tight and attached the covering with pins. With the cleaning finished, she took a clean sheet and spread it over the colonel. Sarah made another trip downstairs with the dirty pan of water and old bandages. She returned to the bedroom and turned down the lamp as low as possible, pulled a large easy chair close to the bed, and sat down to rest.

West Point, on the banks of the beautiful Chattahoochee River, started out in the early 1800s as a trading post . The owners traded calico, sugar, blankets, and other necessities to the Indians and settlers. A few log cabins were built, and farmers began to grow crops. They named the town Franklin, and over time it grew into a small community. That the town grew successfully into a thriving community was due to a mistake. The West Point Railroad Company decided to extend their rail line from Atlanta to Franklin and then on south to Columbus, Georgia. The rails would also be extended east from Montgomery, Alabama, and meet at Franklin. Plans were for the town to become a transportation center and cotton market. The rail lines were laid and the tracks were completed in 1854. It was around this time the town found there was already a town named Franklin, so they changed the name to West Point.

It was quickly discovered that the two tracks from Montgomery and Atlanta could not be joined. The tracks from Montgomery were two inches closer together than those from Atlanta. The solution was to transfer passengers and freight from each line on every run from the two cities. Although this was an inconvenience, it contributed greatly to the growth of West Point. The town quickly became a transportation center, and there was rapid growth in the warehouse and hotel business. At the outbreak of the Civil War, West Point built two hospitals and became a place to send wounded Confederate soldiers to rest and convalesce.

It was just after dawn when Sarah awoke, still in the chair beside her bed. She was momentarily startled that a man was in her bed, but quickly recovered when she remembered the events of the previous day. She remained still for several minutes, saying a small prayer that the soldier beside her was still alive. Slowly she stood and bent over his face, just inches from him, as she listened to make sure he was breathing. She looked into his closed eyes, and just at that moment his eyes opened widely. Neither moved or spoke for several seconds as they stared at each other, until finally, the colonel asked softly, "Am I in Heaven?"

"Almost," replied Sarah. "You're in West Point, Georgia."

"I thought you were an angel," he said.

She moved back as he frowned, trying to remember what had happened. Then it all came back to him. As he remembered the events of the battle, he reached down to feel for the missing leg, and realized that it had not been a dream. It had happened. He closed his eyes and grimaced in pain.

"You are going to be fine. I'm going to get you some water. I'll be right back," she said, as she hurried downstairs.

She returned quickly with a glass of cold water and held the glass to his lips. He raised his head from the pillow and drank. When he had finished, he dropped his head back and sighed.

"How did I get here?" he asked.

"They brought you and several other wounded soldiers here last evening. You were unconscious, so I had them bring you up here. My name is Sarah Bradford, and this is my home."

"My name is Robert Tyler, Colonel, Confederate Army of Tennessee," he said. "It's an honor to meet you. I apologize for being such a burden, and thank you for your gracious hospitality."

"Well, you are welcome, Colonel Tyler, and you are welcome to stay here while you recuperate from your wound," she said. "Unless you need something right now, I'm going to go down to the kitchen and fix you something to eat. You were on the road for two days without any food."

Tyler nodded his head in agreement, and Sarah turned and went down the stairs. She said a small prayer of thanks that her patient was alive and awake.

CHAPTER SEVEN

It was mid-morning and Sarah was working in the kitchen when she heard a knock at the back door. Looking out the window, she saw that it was her best friend, Elizabeth Steele.

"Hi, Liz, come on in," she said as she opened the back door.

"What will it be this morning, hot or iced tea? Let's sit at the breakfast table," she said, as she pulled out two chairs.

"Hot tea would be nice, Sarah," Elizabeth replied as she sat down.

Elizabeth and Sarah shared a special feeling of loss and sorrow. Like Sarah, she also had the unfortunate distinction of losing her husband to the war. William Steele was killed at the Battle of Antietam, near Sharpsburg, Maryland, on September 17, 1862, the bloodiest day of battle in American history. More men were killed or wounded on this date than on any other single day of the Civil War. Federal losses were 12,410, and Confederate losses 10,700, although neither side gained a decisive victory.

"I saw them carry one of the wounded soldiers into your house last evening, and I was wondering how he was doing."

Sarah put a finger to her lips, and replied in a low voice, "He's upstairs in bed. He was unconscious when they brought him in, but he came to this morning."

Elizabeth spoke in a low voice, "What are his injuries?"

"He lost a leg just below the knee, but the wound appears

to be healing. If he doesn't get gangrene, I believe he will survive."

Sarah went over to the stove and picked up the pot of hot tea and brought it and a plate of cookies to the table. Again, speaking softly she said, "He appears to be very sad over the loss of his leg. I do hope his outlook will improve as his body mends."

They both ate cookies and drank their tea in silence for a few minutes.

"This infernal war has been such a disaster for everyone. I just hope it ends soon," sighed Elizabeth.

"I know, I know. It has brought so much sadness and misery; I just don't know how much more we can take," said Sarah, as she slowly stirred her tea and stared into her cup.

Colonel Tyler slept most of the first day at Sarah's house, and the rest and food greatly improved his color and energy. When he was awake, he worried about being such a burden, and when Sarah returned to the bedroom with dinner the second day, he decided to mention it to her.

"Mrs. Bradford, I am most grateful for all the care you have provided. It has done wonders for my health and recuperation. However, I feel I cannot continue to impose on you and be such a burden. I believe it would be best if I was moved to one of the local hospitals for my care."

Sarah was taken aback for a moment by his suggestion to leave the house, but quickly recovered.

"Colonel Tyler, I want you to know that you are neither

a burden nor an imposition on me. I have volunteered to provide support and assistance in your recovery and consider it a small contribution to the cause. Besides, the two convalescing hospitals here are completely full of wounded soldiers and could not take another patient at this time."

"Mrs. Bradford, I thank you for all the care you have provided, but I fear it will take some time for me to fully recover, and I will continue to be an imposition to you."

"Please call me Sarah. I will hear no more of you leaving this house. You should know that I am here alone, and I will enjoy having you here for company and conversation."

"I will use your first name, only if you agree to call me Robert. And at your insistence, I will stop any talk of moving out. You mentioned you live here alone. May I be so bold to ask you about your husband?"

"My husband, Henry, fell on December 31, 1862, at the Battle of Stones River, near Murfreesboro, Tennessee."

"I am so sorry for your loss. Please accept my apology for an insensitive question."

"That's all right. It's a question I have had to answer many times before. Now, Robert, it's settled. You will recuperate here in my house, and, in turn, I will enjoy your company."

"So be it, Sarah. The subject is closed, and now I will sleep." Tyler smiled slightly and dropped his head back onto the pillow and closed his eyes.

"Good night, Robert," said Sarah. She picked up the tray and went downstairs.

When Elizabeth arrived the next morning for her visit and tea, Sarah had already fed Robert breakfast and was in the kitchen cleaning the dishes. They sat at the breakfast table and had tea and biscuits.

"Liz, would you like to meet my patient today? I believe he has recovered enough for a visitor, and it may do him some good. He seems to be depressed over his condition."

"Yes, I would, Sarah, if you feel I am not imposing on him."

"I'll go up and see if he is agreeable for a visitor."

Sarah went upstairs and returned in a few minutes. "He said it would be fine to visit, but to warn you that he will not be able to stand like a proper gentleman."

They went upstairs, and Sarah gently knocked at the door before entering.

"Robert, I would like for you to meet my very best friend, Elizabeth Steele. Elizabeth, I would like to introduce you to Colonel Robert Charles Tyler."

"It is my pleasure to meet you, Mrs. Steele. Please accept my apology for not standing."

"It is an honor to meet you, Colonel Tyler," said Elizabeth.

"Robert, Elizabeth lives next door, and we have known each other for seven years. Regrettably, like me, she also lost her husband in the war."

"Yes, Charles was killed at the Battle of Antietam."

"I'm sorry for your loss, Mrs. Steele."

"Thank you, Colonel. You will find that just about every family here at West Point has lost someone, either a father, husband, or son. The war has devastated our town. But we still have the will and strength to withstand our losses and go forward. We are particularly proud that we have our two hospitals and can contribute to the war effort by providing support to the soldiers as they recuperate from their wounds. I work at one of the hospitals and see the results of our efforts every day."

"On behalf of the Army of the Confederacy, I thank you for your support. Your work is a Godsend to the cause."

"Thank you, Colonel. As Sarah mentioned, I'm just next door if you ever need anything. With Sarah's care, you are in very capable hands. I am so pleased to meet you, and will leave now and let you rest."

"It was my pleasure meeting you, Mrs. Steele."

Sarah and Elizabeth went back downstairs to the kitchen.

"Sarah, you didn't tell me you had captured a colonel, and that he is handsome," gushed Elizabeth.

Sarah blushed. "Now, Liz, I had no choice in the matter. He was the last of the wounded, and I could not refuse to provide aid to him. But I have to agree—he is quite handsome."

"And you already have him in your bed," Elizabeth said, with a laugh.

Sarah's face began to get red from embarrassment.

"Now, Liz, I only had one large bed, and I had to put him where he would be comfortable."

Elizabeth continued to laugh. "I understand, Sarah," she said as she started for the door. "I had better leave you now, so that you can tend to your colonel."

CHAPTER EIGHT

For several days Tyler had laid in bed and contemplated his future. He was gradually improving physically, due in large part to the ministrations of Sarah. Tyler's mental condition, on the other hand, was deteriorating. With nothing to distract him, he constantly fretted over the fact that he was now disabled, an invalid with an uncertain future. He had always been fiercely independent and self-reliant, but now he had to depend on others for even the most basic necessities. He stared at the ceiling of the bedroom and frowned as he considered a bleak future. There was a knock at the door, and Sarah entered the room.

"Colonel Tyler, there's a young gentleman here that would like to speak to you," she said.

"Who is it, and what does he want?" asked Tyler in a gruff voice.

"It's William Chastain, a local young man, and I believe he has something for you."

"Well, I guess you should show him in then."

Sarah opened the door and a young boy of fourteen entered the room, carrying a large piece of wood. He stopped at the end of the bed and, obviously nervous, addressed Tyler.

"Colonel Tyler, it's an honor meeting you sir. My name is William Chastain, although most people just call me Willie." He stopped speaking and swallowed.

Tyler stared at him with a slight frown and remained silent.

"Sir, I heard about your ailment from your recent fighting

with the Yankees, so I made something that you might find useful for support." Willie raised the piece of wood that he had brought with him. "I whittled this as an aid to help support you with your walking." Willie made sure he didn't call it a crutch or refer to Tyler's amputated leg.

Tyler raised up in the bed as Willie handed the crutch to him. It was easy to see that he had spent a lot of time making it. The wood was smooth and polished and the branch formed a natural Y shape. Willie had fitted a horizontal piece to fit under his arm and a smaller piece for his hand further down. Tyler took the crutch from Willie and looked it over from end to end, continuing to frown as he inspected it. Sarah and Willie stood at the end of the bed, anxiously awaiting his comment. Looking at Tyler, they could not know it, but his mind was racing. He quickly realized that with this crutch he would no longer be an invalid. With some practice, he would be able to move around and carry out normal activities. He recalled seeing other soldiers who had lost an arm or leg that were able to continue their military careers. He had experienced a misfortune, but it would not keep him down. After several minutes of inspecting the crutch, Tyler looked up at Sarah and then at Willie. A broad smile lit up his face as he said, "Willie, this is the best gift I have ever been given. You may never realize how much it means to me. I accept it with much gratitude."

Sarah and Willie let out their breaths and smiled.

"Now, Willie, what may I do for you in return for this magnificent gift?" asked Tyler.

Willie gulped and said, "Well, Colonel Tyler, I tried to enlist in the Confederacy, but they said I was too young, that

I should wait another year. But I want to do something now for the South. Colonel, if you would see fit, I would like to volunteer to be your unofficial aide while you are here at West Point." Willie stopped speaking and stared at Tyler.

"Willie, I would be honored to have you be my unofficial aide, and I'm sure your assistance will prove to be of great value."

Sarah smiled and clasped her hands together, and Willie grinned broadly.

"Thank you, Colonel Tyler. I'll leave now, but will stop by each day and report to you." He saluted and went out the door.

"Well, Sarah, it looks like I have some work to do, learning how to use this thing to support me as I get around."

"I'm sure it will work just fine," she said with a smile.

The day after Willie's visit, Sarah prepared breakfast as usual and took a tray up to Tyler's bedroom. She knocked on the door and entered, noting Robert seemed to be in good spirits as he positioned himself in a sitting position in the bed, and she placed the tray in his lap. Sarah noticed the crutch leaning on the side of the bed, but neither mentioned it as they made small talk while he ate his meal. When he was finished eating, Sarah gathered up the tray and took it downstairs.

After Sarah left the room, Tyler began to plan how he was going to get up and move around the room on his first attempt at walking. He knew that the first steps might be awkward and resigned himself to limit his activities to just moving about the room at first. He took the crutch and leaned it on the side of the bed where it would be easily available. Next, he folded his blanket and sheet to the other side of the bed so they would be out of the way. As he was dressed only in a long night shirt, his clothing should not get in his way. Tyler's plan was to sit up, scoot his body down to the middle of the bed, then rotate his leg over the side. Then, with the support of the crutch, he would try to stand up. He made the first move with no problem, but when he swung his leg over the side of the bed, he became lightheaded and the room seemed to spin. He placed both hands at his sides on the bed, and after remaining motionless for a few minutes, the room stopped spinning. Good, so far, he thought, but the next move might prove more difficult. He grabbed the crutch and placed it on the floor for support. He slid his good leg onto the floor, then with a heave, lifted his body off the bed. He was now standing in the middle of the room, but unexpectedly, once again the room seemed to spin. In an attempt to regain his balance, he picked up the crutch and set it down with a loud thump. He began to lose his footing as his body turned, and he started to fall. As he went down, he saw the easy chair and grabbed one of its arms, which helped him guide his body into the chair, and he fell into it in a sitting position. Meanwhile, he had let go of the crutch, and it fell to the floor, making a loud noise.

Sarah was in the kitchen, washing the dishes, when she heard the noise upstairs. She thought something terrible must have happened to Robert, and she ran up the stairs and threw open the door. She first looked at the empty bed, then to the chair where Tyler was sitting. They stared at each other for a minute, neither speaking.

"I decided to get out of bed," Tyler finally said.

"So I noticed," replied Sarah, with a sigh. "Are you all right?" she asked.

"I'm fine, but I think I'll remain here for a time," said Tyler.

"That sounds like a good idea," Sarah said. She picked up the crutch and handed it to Tyler.

"I believe my new way of walking will require some getting used to," said Tyler.

"I'm going back downstairs. Call me if you need anything," she said, as she walked out and closed the door. She breathed a small sigh of relief.

Although it had not gone quite as he planned, Tyler was pleased that he had managed to get himself out of bed. For the next two days, he practiced getting in and out of bed several times and was confident that he could accomplish this task without assistance. He was even able to take a few steps, with the aid of his walking staff. His next move would be more difficult, and he realized he would need some help.

When Sarah brought breakfast the next morning, Tyler mentioned to her his ability to get in and out of bed. "Sarah, I need to keep progressing if I am going to one day be completely mobile," he said. "My next challenge is to be able to get down and then back up the stairs. I would like to try that today if you will help me."

"I would be glad to assist you, Robert. I'll take the breakfast dishes down and come back up in a few minutes," she said, as she picked up the tray and went downstairs. When she returned, she was surprised that he was already out of bed and standing in the middle of the bedroom.

"Sarah, I think it would work best if you went first, and I'll use your shoulder for support and my walking staff for balance."

Sarah nodded in agreement, and they proceeded very slowly out the bedroom door to the landing at the top of the stairs. She stopped, and Tyler placed his hand on her shoulder. She felt a warm, pleasant sensation from his touch.

"All right, now let's try the first step," Tyler said.

Sarah moved very slowly down the first step, and Tyler, with his hand on her shoulder, moved down the stairs without mishap. They proceeded slowly, step by step down the stairs without an accident. Tyler was smiling and visibly pleased. They remained at the bottom of the steps for a few minutes and rested.

"All right, now let's see if we can reverse the procedure and return upstairs."

Tyler led the way, with Sarah following closely behind, so that he could use her shoulder for support. They successfully returned up the stairs to the bedroom. Tyler collapsed in the large easy chair and took a deep breath.

"Do you think we could practice again this afternoon, Sarah?" he asked.

"Of course, Robert, just let me know anytime you want my assistance. You stay there for a while and rest, and I'll return with something to drink." Sarah left the room smiling, happy that Robert was doing so well, and pleased that he was relying on her to help him.

Tyler was happy about his progress in moving around, and now that he could get up and down the stairs, he realized that he needed to be able to walk and turn in order to be completely mobile. With this in mind, he developed a plan for practicing. When Sarah brought breakfast up the next morning, he mentioned it to her.

"Sarah, I've made a plan to practice my walking so that I will be completely mobile. Now that I can get up and down the stairs with no problems, I plan to go out the back door and practice walking in the back yard."

"Is there anything I can do to assist you?" she asked.

"No, I think I can handle it myself, and I plan to go outside later this morning."

"Well, just let me know if I can help," she said.

Just as he had said, Tyler came down the stairs later that morning, but this time, instead of turning around and going back up, he turned the other way and went out the back door. Once outside, he stood a few minutes, just breathing in the fresh air. He was happy to be outside once again. He decided he would take about fifty steps, then turn around and return to where he had started. He planned to do this each day, until he was confident he could do it naturally. Taking his time, he proceeded to walk.

Willie had come to the house, and he and Sarah watched out the window as Tyler ambled forward. Everything was going well, until he reached the end of his walk and started to turn around. He attempted to make a complete turn in the other direction, but lost his balance. Tyler tried to use the crutch to recover his balance, but it went flying in the other direction. He continued to fall and landed in a heap. Willie bolted for the door to go help, but Sarah stopped him.

"No, Willie, don't go out there," she said.

"But Mrs. Bradford, he needs help," Willie replied.

"I know, I know, Willie. But he must do this himself. He doesn't want to rely on others for help."

Willie and Sarah watched as Tyler reached over and pulled his crutch to him, then used it to get up. When he was upright, he took a minute to brush himself off, then started walking back toward the house. This time when he reached the house and started to turn around, he took his time. Instead of trying to complete the turn in one move, he did a partial turn, and then another. Everything went well, and he continued his practice. After thirty minutes of walking, he entered the back door of the house.

Sarah went to him and asked, "How did your practice go, Robert?"

"It went very well, Sarah. I just need to keep practicing until I can move with complete confidence and agility. My plan is to practice at least twice a day until I am satisfied with my ability to move and walk."

"Now are you ready for something to drink?"

"That would be great," he replied.

CHAPTER NINE

Elizabeth continued to tease Sarah about her handsome patient, and Sarah always countered with the explanation that she had no choice in the matter. To herself, though, Sarah acknowledged that she was growing more fond of Robert each day. It was so pleasant to have someone else in the house to talk to and care for. It had been a long time since she had been happy, and now she looked forward to evenings spent sitting on the porch talking with him. She thought Robert had feelings for her, but she was not sure how strong they were. Her biggest worry was that one day he would leave West Point and return to the war. She didn't want to think about him leaving and her not knowing how he felt about her, so she decided that she would ask him that evening. After dinner, she and Robert sat on the porch until it was dark. They retired to their bedrooms, and Robert was reading when he heard a knock on the door.

"Come in," he said.

Sarah entered the room. She was in her nightgown and carried a tray with two glasses of wine. "I found some port and thought you might enjoy a taste," she said as she moved to the side of the bed and sat down.

"That would be fine," he said as he took one of the glasses.

He took a sip and said, "This tastes great, Sarah."

Sarah sipped her wine, and then turned to face Robert directly.

"I've been wanting to talk to you for some time, Robert,

but just didn't know how to say it, so I thought I would just come right out with it now."

"Go ahead, Sarah."

"Robert, it's been such a joy having you here in the house and being able to care for you. I've been alone for so long now, having your company makes each day one that I look forward to."

"It's been such a pleasure for me, too, Sarah. I've never had someone that cared for me like you have. You are spoiling me to no end."

Sarah took one of his hands in hers. "I want you to know that I have grown very fond of you, and now I have very deep feelings for you, and I want to know if you have feelings for me."

"Sarah, I've never been close to anyone before, and I can't be sure what love feels like, but I do know that when I'm with you, I am the happiest I have ever been in my life. When you're not here, I wait anxiously for your return. Every moment with you is a joy."

Sarah placed her glass on the nightstand and took his glass and placed it beside hers. She moved closer to him.

"Robert, I'm so glad to hear you care for me, too." She turned her face to his, and they kissed.

"I've wanted to do that for so long," he said.

"And I have wanted you to do so."

Sarah looked Robert in the eyes and said, "Robert, I have an idea. My bed downstairs is very small and uncomfortable. This bed is soft and large enough for two. I propose we share this one."

Robert smiled and said, "I think that's a great idea," and they sealed their agreement with another long kiss and hug.

Sarah got up and turned down the lamp. She went to the other side of the bed, took off her nightgown, and as Robert turned back the covers, she slipped into the bed and his waiting arms.

Evenings were Sarah's favorite time of the day. She and Robert would sit in rocking chairs on the veranda and sip tea as they watched night approach. They would often make small talk, but there were times when they remained silent as they watched lightning bugs fly over the grass, making small flashes as they moved. Crickets and frogs would chime in with their evening sounds.

But this evening, Sarah was anxious to talk. She began with a statement. "More wounded soldiers arrived today. It seems they are arriving in increasing numbers and frequency lately, and the stories they tell about the war are not good. It appears that the Confederacy is losing most of the battles. It doesn't look at all promising for the cause, does it, Robert?"

Tyler gazed out over the town for several minutes before replying. "No, Sarah, it doesn't look favorable for the South at all."

"Robert, we're going to lose the war, aren't we?"

"Unless there is some miracle by God, in all likelihood, we will lose," he replied. "The North has managed to blockade all the southern ports, and we are running out of vital supplies. We can't even export our cotton to trade for iron ore and ammunition. The North has so many more men available to fight than we have here in the South; it becomes more futile to attempt to match their numbers."

"If the war is over slavery, why don't we just give up the slaves and quit?" she asked.

"While slavery is a major issue, there is much more at stake with this war. I abhor the very idea that one human can own another. The very thought is repugnant to my senses, and I believe to most other God-fearing people. Our founding fathers expressed their opposition to slavery in the Declaration of Independence with the words 'all men are created equal, with unalienable rights of life, liberty, and the pursuit of happiness.' I have always believed that even without this war, it was just a matter of time before all states would abolish slavery. You could see more and more states and territories were becoming free-holding even before the war started."

Sarah and Robert sat in silence for several minutes, and then Sarah spoke. "Robert, if the question of slavery is not the overriding issue of this war, what is it?"

"It's states' rights, Sarah. It's about the right of each state to have state sovereignty. That means each state has the right to decide its future. For years now, the federal government has placed a stranglehold on the southern states by placing tariffs or high import taxes on agriculture goods to protect western farmers, on textiles to protect New England, and on iron ore to protect Pennsylvania. For southern states, the import taxes have been as much as fifty percent, and these states feel that this tax is unauthorized. When the states ratified the Constitution, they gave the federal government specific limited powers and stated that all other power was reserved for the individual states. Our founding fathers knew that all government seems to have an insatiable appetite for power and control. That's why they took great pains to specifically limit the powers given to the government by the states. These powers were very distinct and very limited. This war must reassert the sovereignty of states' rights, or the federal government will continue to eat away at our liberty, and the rights of states will continue to erode. If the South does not succeed, I feel there will come a day when even as the Negro slave is freed, we will all, black and white, become enslaved to the government. Just as in Deuteronomy where it states that one tenth of all our possessions belongs to God, there will come a day when the federal government will assert that one tenth of all our earnings belongs to the government. Heaven forbid that one day government will declare it has the right to decide where we can go and what we can do. This war must reestablish our individual freedoms."

After such a passionate and forceful statement, neither Sarah or Robert spoke. They were both considering how important the states' rights issue was for America's future, and what would happen to their rights if the South did lose the war.

CHAPTER TEN

Tyler was pleased with his medical condition. His leg was healing nicely, and with the aid of his walking staff, he could see steady improvement in his ability to move about. He was anxious to get back to the Confederacy and fighting with the troops. He decided to send a message to General Bragg to see if he could be useful to the army in some capacity. Tyler was able to borrow a horse and sent one of the recuperating soldiers to carry a message to the general. Although the telegraph was available to him, it was notorious for having messages intercepted by the Yankees. Tyler drafted a note stating that his leg would soon be fully mended and that with the aid of his walking staff, he was sufficiently mobile to return to military duty. The messenger left for the trip to Tennessee, but after nearly a week, he had not returned. Tyler began to worry that perhaps he had been killed or captured. On the eve of the sixth day, as Tyler sat on the front porch, his messenger rode up to the house and dismounted. As the messenger came up the steps, Tyler said, "Soldier, I am so pleased to see you return safe and sound. Were you able to find General Bragg and deliver my message?"

"Yes, Colonel Tyler, I had to skirt around some Yankee soldiers a couple of times, but I did deliver your note to the general, and he sent a message back to you. Here it is." The soldier took a paper out of his pocket and handed it to the colonel. Tyler took the paper, carefully unfolded it, and began to read:

Confederate Army of Tennessee
May 23, 1864

My Dear Colonel Tyler:

I am extremely pleased to hear that you are on the mend and recovering from your wound. It is with profound regard and pleasure that in response to your demonstrated leadership and courage in battle, I have recommended and President Davis has authorized your permanent promotion to Brigadier General, Army of the Confederate States of America, this date, May 8, 1864.

Braxton Bragg, General Commander

There was a second message for Colonel Tyler:

Brigadier General Robert C. Tyler,

You are herewith ordered to command the services of all able bodied soldiers in your immediate area in defense of the vital transportation railroads and rail services located at West Point, Georgia. May God be with you and the Confederate States of America.

General Braxton Bragg
Commander, Army of Tennessee

Tyler was overwhelmed for a moment. He had just received a promotion and orders back to duty and command. He stared out at the town as many thoughts ran through his mind.

"There's one other thing, sir," said the soldier.

"Yes, what is it?"

"General Bragg told me to give you this," and the soldier pulled a small pouch from his front pocket. Tyler took the pouch and opened it and picked out two silver stars.

"General Bragg said to tell you he wore these in his first general-grade promotion, and he would be honored if you also wore them."

Tyler smiled at the soldier and said, "You have done a good job and deserve some rest. Thank you. You are dismissed."

The soldier saluted and turned away.

Tyler sat down and began to think of all the things he needed to do.

Sarah worked part-time at McDougall's warehouse counting goods and making entries in the large inventory ledgers. She didn't mind the work because it was relatively easy, the wages helped out with running her house, and the warehouse was within easy walking distance from her home.

When she returned home that evening, Tyler was already sitting on the porch. He appeared in a good mood and asked her if she had a good day. Sarah remarked that everything had gone well and went into the house, got iced tea for them, and returned to the porch. When she was seated, she asked Tyler how his day had gone.

"It went just fine, Sarah, and I have some great news to share with you. Today, I received a message from General Bragg. I have been promoted to brigadier general, and I also received orders for my next duty assignment."

"Oh, Robert, the promotion is great news, but please don't tell me you will be leaving."

"No, Sarah, that's some more good news. My orders are to assemble a fighting force and defend the rail lines here at West Point."

Sarah sighed with relief. "Robert, I am so happy you will not be leaving. I don't think I could stand it if you left, and I was all alone. I need you to be here with me."

"I will not leave you, Sarah. I feel the same way about you. I would be heartbroken if we had to part."

He took her hand in his, and they sat silently for several minutes.

"I do have a favor to ask, Sarah. I have asked Captain Gonzalez to act as my second-in-command and to gather all able-bodied soldiers here tomorrow morning. I would be honored if you would take part in my promotion ceremony."

"Thank you, Robert, for including me. I wouldn't miss it for anything."

The next morning at 8:00 a.m., Captain Gonzalez had 270 soldiers assembled in front of Sarah's house. The men were all recuperating from various wounds, but Gonzalez thought they were sufficiently recovered to assist in defending the town.

Sarah and Tyler walked out the front door, and the Captain called the men to attention. He did an about face and saluted Tyler, then took a paper from his pocket and began to read:

Attention to orders, by direction of Jefferson Davis, President of the Confederate States of America, and General Braxton Bragg, Commander, the Confederate Army of Tennessee, on this date, May 8, 1864, Robert Charles Tyler is promoted to Brigadier General, Army of the Confederate States of America.

Captain Gonzalez took the two silver stars from his pocket and handed one to Sarah. As Tyler stood at attention facing the formation of soldiers, the captain pinned a star on one of Tyler's shoulders, and Sarah did the same on the other shoulder. Captain Gonzalez returned to a position in front of the formation facing Tyler and saluted the general. Tyler returned the salute. The captain took two steps backward, and Tyler looked out at the men and gave them the order, "Stand at ease."

The general began to address the formation: "Gentlemen, you are here this morning because I asked Captain Gonzalez to assemble every able-bodied man in the vicinity of West Point. In addition to my promotion, I have also received orders from General Bragg to take charge of every soldier in this area and defend West Point, its railroads, bridges, and warehouse goods. I have developed a plan for a fortification, but it will take some hard work to accomplish. I am now asking each of you to contribute to this mission as much as you are physically able. However, if you do not feel that you can provide any assistance, you are free to leave the formation at this time without fear of castigation or retribution."

The general stopped talking and waited for a time. Not one person moved from the formation.

"All right, then, I am pleased all of you are joining me. As

I said, I have surveyed the area and developed a plan to construct a fort. If you look behind you to the northwest corner of town, you will see a hill that is about 300 feet high. That is where we will construct our fort. We have three cannons in town, two Napoleon twelve pounders, and a thirty-two pound naval gun. These cannons have a range of 1,800 yards, and from the hill we can use them to protect the roads and bridges. We will need to construct an earthen fort on top of the hill. I will meet with you there tomorrow morning, and we will begin laying out the plans for building the fort. Now, does anyone have a question?"

There were no questions.

"Then, at this time I will return the formation to Captain Gonzalez."

He called the formation to attention, and the captain moved to the front of the men and saluted the general. Tyler turned and went back into the house. He could hear the men cheering "hurrah" and shouting rebel yells.

CHAPTER ELEVEN

At 8:00 the next morning, the men met with General Tyler and Captain Gonzalez at the base of the hill. The general thanked the men for their support and began to tell them of his plans for building the fort: "Men, I've checked the top of the hill, and it is flat and wide. We can build an earthen fort there fairly easily and quickly. I've drawn up a sketch of how it will look when it is completed. The fort will be 100 feet on each of its four sides. We will need to dig a moat six feet wide and six feet deep around all four sides, and we will use the dirt we move for the moat to build a rampart on each of the four sides. This mound of dirt will give us protection when we stand behind it and fire our weapons. We will also need to build a small, covered room in the center of the fort to serve as our magazine where we can safely store our ammunition. One of the twelve pounders will go on the southeast corner and one on the southwest corner, and they will be used to guard the roads leading into town. The thirty-two pounder will go on the northeast corner, and it will protect the railroad bridge across the river. We will build one footbridge to get across the moat that we can draw inside the fort so it will not be available to the enemy. I believe that covers all my plans. Does anyone have any questions?"

No one spoke up.

"If not, then let's get to work. I had Captain Gonzalez procure stakes and rope to lay out the sides of the fort. He has also brought shovels and carts to move the dirt."

All of the men began to move up the side of the hill and

were soon busy digging and moving the earth. Blessed with good weather almost every day, the work on the fort progressed steadily. In two months, the work was nearly finished. The ammunition magazine stood in the center of the fort, and the cannons were in place at the corners of the rampart. General Tyler gathered all the soldiers together and thanked them for all their hard work.

"We have one more thing to do before the fort is finished," he said. "We need to give this fort a proper name. I am open to your suggestions on what to call it."

Captain Gonzalez spoke up. "General, we have all decided on a name, and we think it should be called 'Fort Tyler' in your honor."

General Tyler smiled broadly and said, "Well, then, if that is what you want, Fort Tyler it is!"

All of the men yelled and cheered as the general moved down the hill.

It was a beautiful summer morning as General Tyler and his troops were spread out on the hillside, chopping down brush and small trees so they would have unobstructed lines of fire in the event the Yankees attacked the fort from any direction. One of the soldiers noticed a group of women approaching the hill. He quickly alerted the general, and with no words spoken, the men put down theirs tools and gathered behind him. When the women reached the group, they stopped, and Elizabeth, holding a bundle in her arms, walked up to the general and began to speak.

"General Tyler, some of the women contributed cloth from their window drapes, and we sewed this flag for the fort. We want to present it to you today as a small contribution to your efforts, and as a token of our appreciation for all that your soldiers are doing to defend our town."

The general, deeply moved, took the flag from her.

"Ladies, in the name of the Confederacy, I accept this flag. In return for your sacrifices and thoughtfulness, I make a solemn promise to you today. I pledge to you all that I will protect and defend this flag and all that it stands for until my last breath. Should this fort be attacked while I am here, when this flag is lowered to the ground, you will find my dead body at the foot of its staff."

All of the men standing behind the general applauded and cheered, yelling, "Hurrah for Dixie," but the women remained silent.

For a long moment, they stared at the general. His words had been so forceful and determined, you could see emotions in the women's eyes ranging from fear to sadness. Without a word spoken by them, the women lowered their heads, turned, and walked back down the hillside.

The general turned to the men and said, "Now that we have a proper flag for the fort, we must make a flagpole and position it in a prominent location."

The men cheered again and waved their hats. Then they turned and went back up the hill to continue their work.

General Tyler and Captain Gonzalez traveled north twenty

miles to LaGrange, Georgia, by horseback, reaching the edge of town early in the afternoon. As they guided their horses to the town square and dismounted at the water trough, they saw thirty to thirty-five women coming toward them from several directions. The women were all armed with a variety of pistols and rifles. They formed a loose formation, and one of the women stepped forward to greet the men.

"Lieutenant Mary Heard, Nancy Harts Company, La-Grange First Militia, reporting," she said as she saluted.

General Tyler returned the salute. "It's an honor to meet you. Please tell your troops to stand at ease."

She turned to the group of women and said sharply, "All, stand at ease." The women relaxed, but remained in a group.

"General, we've heard of your presence in West Point, and we are honored with your visit."

"No, no, it's truly my honor to visit the great town of LaGrange and to see such a courageous force of women."

Lieutenant Heard invited the two officers to sit under a large shade tree and have some tea. When they were seated and had their drinks in hand, General Tyler thanked them for the hospitality. With the formalities out of the way, the general began to speak.

"Lieutenant Heard, I have orders from General Bragg to defend the rail lines at West Point, and I am in the process of building a fort overlooking the town and railroad. I heard about your company and thought it would be good to meet you. In the event of attack by the Yankees, it would be a good plan to provide as much support to each other as possible. Now, it's impossible not to see that your troops are all female. Are there any men available here to support you?"

"No, all the town's men are off fighting the Yankees. We do have a few boys around town, but none of them are yet of fighting age."

She nodded at the other women standing by. "I know these ladies may not impress you as fighters, but I can promise you that when the time comes, they will stand up to the Yankees, just like the men."

"I believe you, Lieutenant, but hope that time will never come. Your town has already given much to the cause, and we are very appreciative. I do have one more question: how do you come by the name Nancy Harts Company?"

"General, Nancy Hart was a hero in the Revolutionary War. She hailed from eastern Georgia, and she single handedly captured some English troops about to burn her home. We thought it would be only fitting to name our company after her."

General Tyler visited for a while longer and made a point to meet each one of the women soldiers. Before departing, he promised to stay in contact and provide as much support as possible in defense of their town.

Nancy Anne Morgan was born in 1744, in Orange County, North Carolina. She married Benjamin Hart from Hanover County, Virginia, and they moved to South Carolina and had eight children. Around 1771, they moved to Wilkes County, Georgia, and settled along the Broad River. They were living in Wilkes County when the Revolutionary War began. In describing Nancy Hart, there is no way to make her out as attractive. She was tall, over six feet tall, and gangly. She was rough and raw-boned, with flaming red hair and a smallpox-scarred face. She was also cross-eyed. Her physical appearance was matched by a feisty personal attitude characterized by a hot-headed temper, a fearless spirit, and a desire to demand revenge upon those who offended her or harmed her family and friends. Local Indians referred to her as "Wahatche," which means "war woman." Although illiterate, Hart was blessed with the skills and knowledge necessary for frontier survival. Despite her crossed eyes, she was a skilled hunter and excellent shot. What Nancy Hart lacked in attractiveness, she made up for in her devout patriotism and loathing of the British loyalists or Tories, English soldiers, and British sympathizers. She became Georgia's most active female participant during the Revolutionary War. She often disguised herself as a simple-minded man and wandered into Tory camps and British garrisons and spied on them to gather information, which she passed along to patriot authorities. She was an active participant in the Battle of Kettle Creek, where a group of militiamen attacked the Patriots on February 14, 1775. Over 100 of the enemy were killed, the remainder routed. This battle was the first success for Georgia patriots against the British. On another occasion, six Tories forced themselves into her house and demanded to be fed. They killed one of her turkeys and insisted she cook it. While she did, they drank her corn whiskey and bragged about killing her neighbor, Colonel Danby. Nancy slipped their guns from where they were stacked and hid them in her cabin wall. When they noticed their guns were gone, they rushed her. She grabbed her musket and wounded one of the Tories.

Then she grabbed another musket and killed a second Tory as he ran for his weapon. Nancy captured the remaining Tories and held them until her husband and several other members of the militia returned home. She insisted the captives be hanged for killing her neighbor. It was widely reported they were dragged from the cabin to a tree near a spring and hanged there while Nancy sang "Yankee Doodle."

There are many other stories of Nancy's exploits during the Revolutionary War, and she quickly became a local hero. After the war, she and Benjamin Hart moved to Kentucky, where she died in 1830.

CHAPTER TWELVE

General James Harrison Wilson was a twenty-eight year old brevet (temporary rank) major general serving in the Union army under General Sherman. He was one of a very few soldiers to rise from private to general during the war. In December 1864, General Sherman ordered the "Boy General" to assemble a cavalry force and train them in preparation for a raid through Alabama and Georgia. Much of this area had remained relatively untouched, even in the late stages of the war, and it continued to be vital for shipping and was a major producer of war supplies. Wilson's mission was to destroy this area's ability to supply the Confederacy with military supplies and ammunition. Sherman gave Wilson authority to operate independently, with complete discretion in the conduct of his cavalry operation. In the spring of 1865, after organizing and training several thousand mounted troops armed with new Spencer repeating rifles, 1,500 dismounted troops, 250 supply wagons, and a battery of horse-drawn artillery, Wilson was ready to launch his cavalry operation. Here is an overview of what would be the largest cavalry raid of the Civil War.

March 22, 1865—General Wilson and his Cavalry Corps, Military Division of the Mississippi, departed Gravelly Springs, in the northwest corner of Alabama, heading south.

March 29, 1865—Wilson and the main body of his force had

worked their way to central Alabama, near Birmingham, the heart of the state's iron and coal district. His troops met little resistance, and they made quick work of destroying mills, coal mines, and iron foundries in Oxmoor, Irondale, and the surrounding area.

March 31, 1865—Wilson's forces continued south and routed the Confederate troops and burned the Roupes Valley Ironworks and Bibb Naval Furnace at Montevallo. Upon reaching Tuscaloosa, as a symbolic gesture of their dominance, they burned the University of Alabama, which had been a training ground for militia and Confederate troops.

April 2, 1865—The Union force continued south, and on this date the Battle of Selma took place. Selma was one of the Confederates' last reliable arsenals and housed guns, ammunition, ironworks, foundries, and locomotives. General Nathan Bedford Forrest, the local Confederate commander, attempted to halt Wilson's advance upon Selma at Ebenezer Church, located nineteen miles from the city, but was defeated and forced back into the city's defenses. Wilson quickly overwhelmed Selma's outnumbered and poorly equipped defenders. His troops destroyed the city's military industries, including the arsenal, naval ordnance works, and eleven iron works and foundries.

April 12, 1865—Wilson's troops occupied Montgomery, the first capital of the Confederacy, after meeting very little resistance. Confederate troops that had been defending the city had been ordered to Columbus, Georgia, leaving the capital virtually defenseless. Union troops destroyed the city's arsenal, train depot, foundries, rolling mills, and several riverboats and railroad cars during their two-day occupation. Wilson then headed eastward toward Geogia.

April 15, 1865—From his camp at Auburn, Alabama, Wilson split his force, sending half to Columbus, Georgia, under the command of Colonel Emory Upton. Columbus, the last great Confederate storehouse, was located on the east bank of the Chattahoochee River, and was important on account of its military stores, railroad transportation, gun boats, armories, arsenals, and work shops. The other half of Wilson's force, led by Colonel Oscar La Grange, headed to West Point, Georgia, with orders to capture the warehouses, train depot, all train implements, and railroad bridges.

Brigadier General Robert Charles Tyler

General James H. Wilson

Colonel Oscar H. La Grange

Fort Tyler cemetery gravesites of Confederate General Robert C. Tyler and Captain Celestine Gonzales

Fort Tyler cemetery gravesites of seventeen Confederate soldiers killed in battle on April 16, 1865

Fort Tyler monument

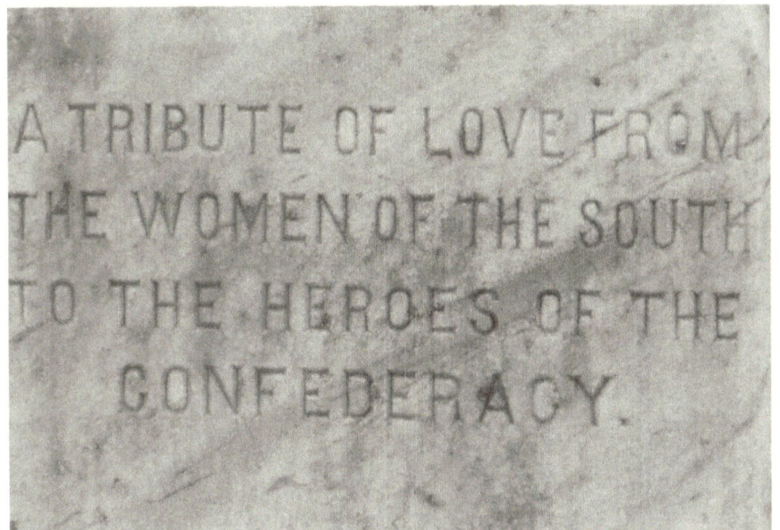

Fort Tyler monument dedication: "A tribute of love from the women of the South to the heroes of the Confederacy."

Fort Tyler monument inscription: "More enduring than marble shall be the memory of the Confederate patriot[s] in whose life fidelity to principle found loftiest expression."

Sixteen pound Napoleon field gun

Thirty-two pound naval gun

Knoll at northwest corner of West Point where Fort Tyler's earthen redoubt field fortification was built

Entrance to Fort Tyler's powder magazine

1776

FORT TYLER

125 yds. northwest, at crest of hill, stood Fort Tyler - last Confederate fort to fall in War Between the States. Fort Tyler was of earthwork construction 35 yds. square surrounded by ditch 12 feet wide, 10 feet deep and enclosed by wooden abatis. The fort was erected to protect important railroad and wagon bridges across Chattahoochee river east of this point.

On Easter Sunday, April 16, 1865, the garrison of 265 Confederates - remnants of Point Coupe Louisiana and Waittes' South Carolina Batteries - aided by boys and convalescent Confederate soldiers - withstood the attack of 3,500 Federals before capitulating late in afternoon. The forces were commanded by Gen. R. C. Tyler, Col. J. H. Fannin, Capts. Gonzales, Trepanier and Webb; Lieuts. Montgomery and McFarland. Units of 2nd and 4th Indiana, 7th Kentucky, and 1st Wisconsin, commanded by Col. O. H. LaGrange, formed part of forces.

Stone home of Dr. A. W. Griggs, Confederate surgeon, built in 1858 (remodeled 1951) stands 40ft. nw. Although hit repeatedly by cannon fire of both forces, original walls are intact. Here Mrs. Griggs and other West Point women gave aid and shelter to wounded of both armies after battle.

Fort Tyler historical marker

FORT TYLER CEMETERY

One hundred feet east in brick walled enclosure are buried 76 brave men, Confederate and Federal, killed or died of wounds in the siege of Fort Tyler.

This engagement occurred April 16, 1865, a whole week after the surrender of General Lee at Appomattox. Only 19 of these graves are marked with names or initials.

In the northeast corner are buried General R. C. Tyler and Captain Gonzales who were killed while commanding the forces defending Fort Tyler against great odds.

Fort Tyler cemetery historical marker

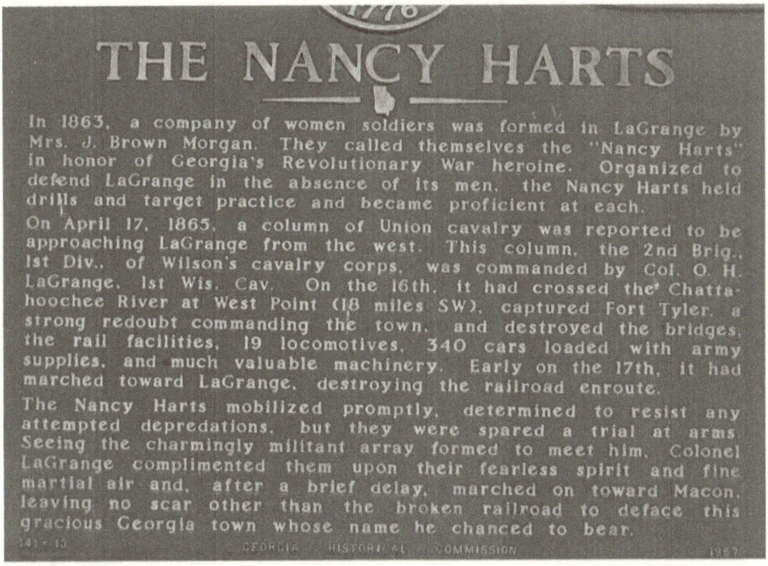

The Nancy Harts historical marker

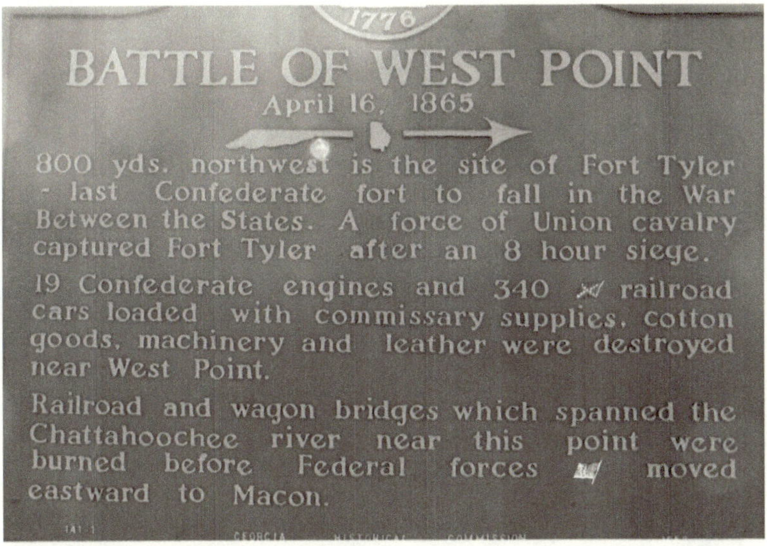

Battle of West Point historical marker

Home of Confederate surgeon A. W. Griggs, located at the southwest corner of Fort Tyler

Railroad bridge across the Chattahoochee River, connecting Alabama and Georgia. The original wooden bridge was destroyed by the Union army.

Two classic historic homes in West Point, Georgia

Two historic homes located at the southeast corner of Fort Tyler

West Point freight depot, built in 1857 and still standing today

CHAPTER THIRTEEN

At 4:15 a.m., Easter Sunday, April 16, 1865, General Tyler and Sarah were awakened from a deep sleep as someone pounded loudly on the front door. They quickly threw robes on over their night clothes and rushed downstairs. It was Willie at the door, excited and nearly out of breath.

"The Yankees are coming, General," he gasped. "Two soldiers just rode in and said there were hundreds of Yankees about twenty miles away, headed in this direction."

Sarah gasped and put her hand to her mouth.

"Willie, I want you to go out front and sound the alarm," the general said. "Tell any soldier you see to go to the fort. I will be there shortly."

"Yes, sir," said Willie, as he ran out to the front yard and began to ring the large bell hanging from a post, giving the signal for an attack.

"Sarah, will you help me get ready?" asked Tyler.

"Of course, Robert," she said, and rushed upstairs to get his clothes.

With her assistance, he quickly got into his uniform. When he was ready to go, they moved to the front door, and he turned to her. He took her in his arms and said, "Sarah, I don't know what my fate will be today, but I know I was destined to lead troops into battle, just as it was meant for us to be together. You must remember that I will always love you and will always be with you."

They stood by the door and hugged each other tightly

for a minute; then he kissed her, turned, and went out the door. Sarah stood there for several minutes, shivering with fear and dread.

By 6:00 a.m., General Tyler had his troops in place, standing behind the parapet with rifles and ammunition. Captain Gonzalez was in charge of the cannons, and he had a crew at each one of the guns. The crews were preparing the cannons for firing and stacking gun powder and canisters loaded with solid shot and shell shot nearby. Everyone waited in quiet anticipation as the sun climbed over the trees and birds began to sing. An alert soldier was the first to notice dust rising in the morning sky to the southwest. Several of the soldiers coughed nervously and spoke to each other in low tones, because they knew the dust cloud was made by the horses of the Union soldiers. It wouldn't be long now before the Yankees were in the town. General Tyler walked up and down the firing lines, speaking softly to the men, telling them to hold their fire until he gave the order and to use their ammunition judiciously. He gave an order to Captain Gonzalez to load the two twelve pounders with solid shot and aim both cannons at the road just at the entrance into town. He told them to be prepared to commence firing at his command. A soldier moved forward and asked the general if they should set fire to the two houses nearby, as they were tall two-story buildings and the roofs would be a good spot for enemy sharpshooters to use to shoot at the men in the fort.

"No, no, those are the Carter and Butler homes. We can't

destroy them; that's all those families have now. We'll just have to be alert and return fire if we get any firing from that direction," said the general.

Now there was nothing more to do but wait.

The men at Fort Tyler watched the cloud of dust grow in size as it moved closer to town. At about 7:30 a.m., General Tyler, using his binoculars, saw the first Union soldiers, the flag bearers, enter the southeast corner of town. They were followed by the cavalry commanders trotting behind the flags, and they, in turn, were followed by the mounted cavalry soldiers.

General Tyler quietly ordered his cannoneers to prepare to fire, as he waited for more of the soldiers to enter the town. Finally, he turned to Captain Gonzalez and gave the order to fire. Gonzalez raised his right arm and swung it down sharply, at the same time giving the order: "Fire!" Both of the twelve pounders made an explosive sound as they belched smoke and recoiled. The battle had begun.

The first rounds landed near the head of the column, knocking Colonel La Grange from his horse, and he hit the ground dazed. After several seconds, he regained his senses and ordered his commanders to have the soldiers dismount and attack on foot. He had his artillery commander bring the artillery guns, forward and soon the Union artillery was trading fire with the Confederate cannons.

Sarah sat in the corner of her living room, watching from a window. The first cannon sounds caught her by surprise. From the loud noise of the guns, she was sure the fighting would be fierce and deadly. Soon she could see Union soldiers running through town, using buildings and homes for cover as they moved steadily toward the fort. There appeared to be hundreds of Yankee soldiers as they continued to advance. Sarah knew then that the men at Fort Tyler were greatly outnumbered, and she had a sickening feeling in her stomach that they could not survive the onslaught. The first cavalry soldiers reached the base of the hill and could see the smoke and fire rising from the cannons. Several sharpshooters entered the two houses nearby and climbed out on the roofs so they could get a position to fire on the men in the fort, and bullets began to whistle past the soldiers standing behind the ramparts.

It was at this moment that Willie came running up the hill and crossed the bridge, entering the fort on a run. With the flag in his hands, he ran up to General Tyler, saluted and said, "General, we need to hoist the flag." Without stopping, he continued to the base of the flagpole and began to climb to the top. Many of the soldiers stopped shooting and watched as he reached the top of the flagpole. With bullets whizzing by, he attached the flag, and then, holding on with one hand, he waved a salute to the union gunners, then slid back down to the ground. All the men in the fort cheered and yelled. Willie ran back up to the general, and smiled as he said, "Now we're ready to fight, sir." Suddenly, a hole appeared in his forehead. He fell to the ground dead, hit by one of the sharpshooters from a rooftop. Willie had become the first casualty of the battle. Two soldiers ran up and moved his body to a corner of the fort. General Tyler was momentarily shocked by what had just transpired. He recovered quickly and shouted for the men to direct their fire to the rooftops of the two houses.

For the next two hours, there was intense fighting as the cavalry soldiers attempted an assault up the hill from all sides, but they were continually driven back by the heavy return fire from the men behind the rampart. Captain Gonzalez had repositioned the two twelve pounders and was now firing grapeshot directly down the hill at the enemy. Colonel La Grange ordered his commanders to have the troops retreat to the base of the hill for a rest before they made a coordinated attack from all sides of the hill. Union soldiers took advantage of the break to cut down saplings and make rough ladders for use in crossing the moat when they reached the top of the hill.

At 10:30 a.m., the attack resumed, starting with the Union artillery concentrating their fire at the cannons and the Yankees storming the hill. One of the first artillery rounds hit one of the cannons, killing the entire crew, including Captain Gonzalez. Union soldiers were making slow progress up the hillsides, even as they received intense fire from behind the ramparts. General Tyler continued to walk behind his soldiers, exposing himself to Union fire, as he rallied his troops to take good aim and conserve their ammunition. At 11:00, as

he stood directly under the flag, General Tyler was hit several times by Union sharpshooters. One round hit his crutch, and several other rounds tore into his body. True to his words, he fell and died under the Confederate flag. The fight continued on for another thirty minutes, when the surviving rebel soldiers realized they were almost out of ammunition and that continuing to fight was useless. They raised a white flag, and the battle was over.

Sarah listened to the sound of the cannons and rifles firing. When it slowed down, then stopped, she knew in her heart that Fort Tyler was lost to the Yankees. By this time, the battle had raged for several hours, and she was numb and weary. She watched out the corner of a window, and after several minutes Union soldiers began to appear as they walked slowly back into town. A few minutes later, she saw smoke rising as the enemy set fire to the locomotives, warehouses, and railroad bridge. Sarah bowed her head and prayed. She knew the worst was yet to come.

CHAPTER FOURTEEN

When the train depot, locomotives, and warehouses had been destroyed, the Union soldiers mounted their horses, and Colonel La Grange led the cavalry through town, continuing east into Georgia. His orders were to take West Point, then proceed on to Macon, where he would link up with Colonel Upton as his force approached from Columbus. Colonel La Grange left 100 soldiers behind at West Point as a burial detail and to guard the Confederate prisoners.

Sarah watched the Union column as it worked its way through town, finally disappearing across the river as it headed east. She continued to sit in the living room and stare out the window, having neither the strength nor the will to move. It had already been a long day, but she anticipated that the worst was yet to come. After another hour, a horse-drawn cart and several Union and Confederate soldiers came slowly down the street, confirming what Sarah had suspected. The cart stopped in front of her house, and two Confederate soldiers came to her door. When she opened it, she could see the sadness in their eyes.

One of the soldiers spoke, "Ma'am, I dread to inform you, but the general was killed in the fighting today. We have his body in the wagon and want to know: will you prepare him for burial?"

Sarah put a hand to her mouth and fell back against the door frame. She couldn't speak for a moment, then replied. "Yes, please bring his body in and place it on the kitchen table."

The soldiers went back to the cart, and several of them used a stretcher to carry the general's body into the house. Sarah held the door open, but couldn't look as they entered. After they had placed the body on the table, one of the soldiers said, "We'll come back in a little while to get the general. Burial services will be this evening."

Sarah stood in the middle of the room, took a deep breath, and told herself that she had to be steadfast for what needed to be done. She recalled several years before, just before Henry left for the war, he made her promise to always be strong and continue on after he was gone. She had tried to keep her promise, but this was so much to bear. She went over to Robert's body and looked at his face. Fortunately, it had no marks, and he looked like he was asleep and at rest. She took his hand in hers, placed it to her face, and stood that way for a long time. Her eyes filled with tears as she continued to tell herself she must be firm. Finally, after a long time, she made herself move. She knew they would return soon for his body, and it had to be prepared for burial. She went upstairs and got a clean shirt and trousers, then went to the kitchen and got water and a wash cloth. Sarah washed Robert's hair and face, kissing his lips gently as she finished. Next, she cut off his shirt, and saw where three bullets had entered his body. She washed the blood from his chest and replaced his shirt and trousers. After combing his hair, she sat beside his body, taking his hand in hers, recalling all the times they had shared. Later that afternoon, the soldiers returned to take him away. They told Sarah that burial services would be at sunset.

As Colonel La Grange and his troops neared the town of LaGrange, Georgia, two scouts galloped up and saluted him. He had sent these men out earlier to take a look at LaGrange and determine if the town was defended. The scouts approached and saluted,

"Colonel, I have a report on the town," said one of the scouts. "Near as we could tell, there are about sixty armed soldiers, and they appear to have taken up defensive positions, waiting for us to attack."

The colonel was disappointed; he was hoping the town was not defended, and they would not have to fight another battle that day. His men were tired from the fierce encounter at West Point and their travel here to LaGrange after the fight.

"Colonel, there's something else, something I never seen before," said the scout.

"What is that?" asked the colonel, impatiently.

"Well, sir, all the troops appeared to be women, no men at all. And they all have rifles."

"Is that right? Women?" The colonel thought for a minute, then said, "Here's what I want you two to do. Go back to LaGrange under a white flag and tell their leader we mean no harm to them or their town. My men are tired and hungry. If they will provide us vittles and something to drink, we will go on our way and leave their town as it is now. On the other hand, tell them if they refuse my proposal, I swear that we will fight until every one of them is dead, and then we will burn the town until there is nothing left but ashes.

Now, you take this message to them and hurry back with an answer. We will rest here and wait for a reply."

The scouts saluted and galloped off.

Colonel La Grange was hoping his offer would be accepted. He was not anxious for another fight today, and even more important, he did not want word to get around that he had been in a battle with women. In about an hour the scouts returned, smiling as they approached the colonel and saluted.

"Sir, they accept your proposal and said you and your men can come on in and rest while they cook you up a meal like you have never had before."

The colonel was relieved. He told the men to mount up, and they moved out.

When the troops approached the town, they could see the women had already started preparing the meal. Two of the women chased down chickens and quickly wrung their necks. They took them over to a boiling pot of water and dipped them in it and then began plucking the feathers. Other women could be seen baking and preparing vegetables to cook over a large fire.

The colonel halted the troops and dismounted as several of the women stopped what they were doing and came over to him. One of the women stepped forward; it was evident she was in charge. Colonel La Grange saluted her and took off his hat.

"Good day, ladies," he said. "My name is Colonel Oscar Hugh La Grange, and my men are members of the Union Cavalry Corp, Military Division of the Mississippi."

The woman in charge returned his salute and said, "Good

afternoon, Colonel La Grange. My name is Lieutenant Mary Heard, and I am in charge of the Mary Harts Company. I want to welcome you to LaGrange and thank you for your gracious offer to spare our town. As you can see, we have already begun to cook a meal for you and your men. We are cooking fried chicken, dumplings, vegetables, and biscuits, and for dessert we have apple, peach, and rhubarb pies."

"That will be a very fine meal," said the colonel. He knew his men had not had a proper meal in many days, and they would be grateful. "I am curious—how do you come by the name of the Mary Harts?" he asked.

The women looked at each other as Lieutenant Heard replied, "Well, Mary Hart is the name of our town librarian. She is very old and feeble now, and we named our outfit in her honor."

The women all smiled as the colonel remarked at how thoughtful the gesture had been.

"General, I suggest you have your men stack their weapons out of the way over there by that building and rest your horses by the water trough. The men can come over here. We'll bring them tea and fruit wine, and they can sit under the trees while they wait for their meal."

"Lieutenant, that's a good idea. We'll do that right away."

The women looked at each other and smiled as they gave a slight nod. Soon all the soldiers were reclining under the trees, drinking tea and wine. When the food was ready, the women placed it on several tables and dished out a large plate of food to each man. The officers waited off to the side until the soldiers were served, and then they each took a plate.

As everyone settled down to eat their meal, several of the

women began to move slowly in the direction of where the rifles were stacked. Just at that moment, a soldier galloped into town and halted his horse directly in front of the colonel. He dismounted and handed him a message. Colonel La Grange read the note and handed it back to the rider, telling him to take it directly to the detail of soldiers he had left back at West Point.

He stood and faced his men. "Gentlemen, give me your attention. I have a very important announcement."

The women glanced at each other with worried looks.

Sarah walked to the cemetery as the sun began to dip below the horizon. There were nineteen caskets laid out beside burial plots, with General Tyler's and Captain Gonzalez's in the front. Relatives and friends stood beside the caskets, and Confederate and Union soldiers gathered at the rear. Sarah stood in the front next to the general's plot with her head down and one hand on his casket, and Elizabeth stood at her side. The local preacher began the service with a prayer, then talked about this day being Easter Sunday, and how significant the great sacrifices made today were to a great and glorious event on the same Sunday many years ago. The congregation sang several hymns and recited a prayer. It was a short service, and the preacher was making his final remarks as a Union soldier galloped up to the rear of the gathering. The rider went to the Union captain in charge and gave him a note. The captain read the message, then walked to the front of the group and handed it to Sarah. Surprised, Sarah took the note and read it. She stood for a minute, then staggered and fell on the general's casket, as she sobbed and let out a moan. She continued to sob as Elizabeth reached down and took the note from her hand and read it, then turned to the group and read aloud:

April 12, 1865

To all officers and men of the Union Army of the United States of America. By the beneficence of the Almighty, I humbly inform you now that the great struggle has ended. On April 9, of this year, near the town of Appomattox Courthouse, Virginia, General Robert E. Lee, general-in-chief of the Army of the Confederacy, surrendered to General Ulysses S. Grant, Commanding General, Union Army. Gentleman, the War is over, you are to cease all hostile actions immediately and return to your homes.

General William Tecumseh Sherman.

Elizabeth looked up at all the people staring at her and said softly, "The war ended seven days ago."

THE END

EPILOGUE

For some time after the end of the war, there was a general dispute as to the location of the last battle of the Civil War. At one time, it was thought to have been at Selma, Alabama. Later there were reports of battles in Texas, but these proved to be only skirmishes between Federals and former Confederates at Palo Alto, near the mouth of the Rio Grande. There was also some protest against the use of the word "battle" for the fighting at Columbus.

The attacks on Columbus and West Point were along an extended line of the same battle, and they were intended to be made about the same hour on the April 16, 1865. These two places were the keys for the crossing of the Chattahoochee and capture of Georgia along its western border. If the attack at Columbus had not been delayed, it would have been difficult to determine if the last battle of the war was Columbus or West Point. It so happened that West Point had fallen several hours before the final night attack and entry into Columbus.

If anything more is needed for the official recognition that the fighting on the 16th of April at Columbus was the last Civil War battle, it is the report of May 30, 1865 by Major General Upton, who commanded the Cavalry Corps Fourth Division and led the assault on Columbus. In it, he states the final assault was made about 9:00 p.m. by General Winslow's Brigade, and by 10:00 p.m., Columbus—with its vast munitions of war, 1,500 prisoners, and 24 guns—were in Union hands, and that this assault was the closing conflict of the war.

In 1913, Charles J. Swift of the Columbus *Enquirer-Sun* wrote an article on the last battle of the war being fought at Columbus. On December 3, 1913, General Wilson wrote a letter to Mr. Swift, and in it he stated, "I am much obliged to you for your writing of the last battle of the war. There seems to be no grounds left for doubt that Columbus was the last battle of the war."

Another letter written on January 23, 1914, by General Winslow, who fought at Columbus, states, "I understand that you wish me to repeat or affirm what has already been printed in the official records of the Union and Confederate Armies, about the precise date on which the battle before and at Columbus was fought. I have always considered that engagement, by the number present and the results achieved, to be the final battle of the war. If you wish specific information which I can furnish in aid of your rightful contention that the last battle between Union and Confederates was fought on the evening of April 16, 1865, at Columbus, Georgia, I shall be glad to give it."

Fortunately, there was never any dispute that the last Confederate fort involved in a battle was Fort Tyler, and the last Confederate general killed in a battle was General Tyler. In his after-battle report, General Wilson stated that "the attack on Fort Tyler at West Point, concluded at 1:30 p.m., on the same day as that at Columbus. General Tyler, its commanding officer, with eighteen men and officers were killed and twenty-eight severely wounded. The entire garrison consisted in all of 265 men and were captured."

After the battles at West Point and Columbus, "the last great Confederate warehouse," Wilson's forces continued east to Macon, Georgia. On May 10, 1865, a patrol of Wilson's men captured the president of the Confederacy, Jefferson Davis, at Irwinville, in south Georgia. Wilson's patrols also captured Confederate Vice President Alexander Stephens, Georgia Governor Joseph E. Brown, Georgia Senator Benjamin Hill, and the notorious Henry Wirz, commandant of Andersonville prison.

There is some dispute as to the effect of Wilson's raid, the largest cavalry raid of the Civil War, on the final outcome of the war, which had already been determined when General Robert E. Lee surrendered to Union general Ulysses S. Grant at Appomattox Court House, Virginia on April 9, 1865.

There is no question, however, that Wilson's raid was a resounding success and the final episode in the South's Civil War experience. In less than a month, Wilson captured over 6,000 enemy prisoners, destroyed four major Confederate industrial centers, and won a major symbolic victory when his troops occupied the former Confederate capital at Montgomery, Alabama. Wilson had effectively destroyed the South's capacity to supply the Confederacy with military supplies and ordnance.

FOR FURTHER READING

Bowman, John S. *The Civil War Almanac*. New York: World Almanac Publications, 1983.

Foote, Shelby. *The Civil War: A Narrative, Vol. 1: Fort Sumter to Perryville*. New York: Random House, 1958.

Foote, Shelby. *The Civil War: A Narrative, Vol. 2: Fredericksburg to Meridian*. New York: Random House, 1963.

Foote, Shelby. *The Civil War: A Narrative, Vol. 3: Red River to Appomattox*. New York: Random House, 1974.

Graham, Martin. *Great Battles of the Civil War*. Lincoln, Illinois: Publications International, 1989.

Keegan, John. *The American Civil War Almanac*. New York: Alfred A. Knopf, 2009.

Macdonald, John. *The Historical Atlas of the Civil War: A Military History*. London: Cartographica Press, 2009.

McCartney, Laton. *The Teapot Dome Scandal*. New York: Random House, 2008.

Recko, Corey. *Murder on the White Sands: The Disappearance of Albert and Henry Fountain*. Denton, Texas: University of North Texas Press, 2007.

A NOTE ON THE TYPE

The text of this book is set in Adobe Caslon Pro, a digital version of a typeface developed by the English type-founder William Caslon circa 1722–1735. The first original English typeface, Caslon became very popular and soon spread to the American colonies. It was the favorite typeface of the printer Benjamin Franklin, and John Dunlap used it to print the Declaration of Independence. It was in widespread use by the time of the American Civil War. The Adobe version was designed by Carol Twombly.

The titles and headers are set in Linotype's Clarendon LT Standard, a digital typeface based on one registered by the English type designer Robert Besley in 1842. Already popular by the time of the Civil War, Clarendon is perhaps best known for its use, a few years later, in the wanted posters of the American West. The Linotype version was originally designed by Hermann Eidenbenz in 1953.